SCANIA
TRUCKING IN AUSTRALIA

The publisher would like to thank Alexander Corne, Manager of Public Relations, Scania Australia for his encouragement and assistance putting this collection of remarkable Scania trucks together in one book.

Front Cover Photograph
Esperance Freight Lines R730, Road Train, Esperance, WA

(Photographer - Paul Kane)

Rear Cover Photograph
Recycal R620 Road Train, Launceston, Tasmania.

(Photographer - Howard Shanks)

Graphic Design (Howard Shanks)

First Edition
ISBN 978-0-9871830-9-5

Copyright © 2022 Howard Shanks (Tebrakunna Holdings Pty Limited).
All rights reserved. No part of this publication may be reproduced, stored in a retrieval system, or transmitted in any form or by any mean, electronic, mechanical, photocopying, recording, or otherwise, without prior written permission of the publisher.

This book is a collection of excerpts from magazine articles written by Howard Shanks during his tenure as an editor-at-large, and customer testimonial stories supplied by Scania Australia. All the information contained in these articles was correct at the time of their first publication.

Contents

LB80 Restoration 6

L111 Restored 14

T143H Diggin' It 18

Scania Truck Cabin Evolution 22

R560 PBS Double 24

General Access 30

All Wheel Drive XT 38

A Long Haul to the Top 46

R730 in the Hardwood 50

The Good Fuel 55

Pumped Up P380 58

Tonka Truck 64

Custom Scania 68

R730 Floats On 74

Drake Steering Widener 80

Low Logger & Traction 82

The Grain Train 90

Opticruise G33 96

Packing on the Payload 100

Turning Heads 106

Movin On R730 111

Clean & Green 118

Scania Mining Trucks 126

Hub Reduction Diffs Explained 128

Its Hot! Its Hard! & Its Heavy! 134

On the way to the Future 142

Scania: Trucking in Australia

Four decades ago, Tasmanian-based livestock transport operator Kerry Hingston purchased a 1973 LB80 that formed the backbone of his operation. It toiled reliably in his business for over a quarter of a century. Today, after a meticulous restoration, that same truck is still the pride of the fleet.

Kerry Hingston was working on an old tractor in his workshop. He had just turned off the oxy-acetylene torch and placed it on the bench. How are you? He asked with a smile, then added, "it a great day to take photos …

A few weeks before, during Kerry's sixtieth birthday party, his family had presented him with his original truck, a 1973 Scania LB80, that they had spent the past 12 months secretly restoring for the occasion.

Kerry and his wife Louise's two sons, Marcus and Nicholas, help run their livestock and milk haulage business in northern Tasmania. The two boys, together with their staff and key suppliers, had painstaking dismantled the old Scania that was as much a founding member of the Hingston Livestock business as its owners and transformed it back to its former glory.

Although, according to Kerry's wife, Lousie, keeping the restoration project a secret from Kerry at times did present a few challenges. "The boys dismantled the truck last year while Kerry and I were on holiday," Louise recalled. "However, after we returned from holidays, Kerry would ask where the old truck was every couple of weeks, and the boys came up with all sorts of excuses that revolved around needing more room in the workshop.

Although Kerry nearly caught us one time, while he was out running a few errands, he mentioned he would drop in to see the painter who paints our trucks because he thought he might know the whereabouts of the old truck. So I quickly rang the boys to tell them Kerry was on the way to the painters, and between them, they promptly invented a story."

"When Kerry finally arrived at the painters, they'd managed to cover the cabin up, which was in the shop getting painted," Louise said. "Kerry asked the painter if he'd seen or heard of the old truck's whereabouts, and the painter

replied that he thought he'd seen one like it advertised on 'Gumtree' a week or so before. So naturally, Kerry wasn't happy, and all the boys could do was laugh. Nevertheless, in the end, we managed to keep the secret, and he was stunned and a little emotional when we finally presented it to him."

Magazine Advertisement

But, rewind the clock to 1975, when a magazine advertisement caught a young Kerry Hingston's eye. A few weeks later, he made one of the most significant investments in his life, purchasing a second-hand 1973 Scania LB80 with 29325 miles on the clock to tow a single-deck cattle trailer that converted into a two-deck sheep crate.

For the young 17-year-old, that second-hand Scania represented a considerable investment, and while there was no missing, the smile on the young man's face as he eased out the clutch and pointed his newly acquired LB80 Scania down the narrow road to collect his first load of cattle. However, deep inside, he quietly suppressed his trepidation about the risk of that significant investment he'd made in an enterprise with such a precarious grip on certainty.

In the early seventies, Australian trucking predominantly consisted of Australian-built petrol-powered Internationals, Dodges, and the lethargic imported Leylands.

"Mercedes-Benz had released their forward-control LPS 1418 in 1968, and by the early seventies, they were gaining

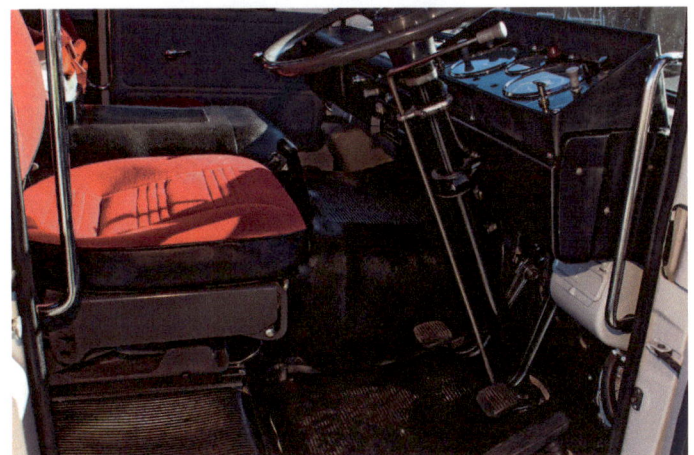

Top Right: The combination instrument, housed the Oil & Coolant Temperature, Fuel and Air pressure gauges as well as a series of warning and indicator lights.
2nd Top Right: Even in the 70s Scania tachos included a green band to show the best engine RPM range.
3rd Top Right: The flat dash panel with the large gauges provided driver with a simple uncluttered cockpit area.
Bottom Right: The interior of the LB80 was neat, orderly and practical with durable rubber floormats.

Opposite Page
Slide-1: Left to Right; Marcus, Katie, Nicholas, Louise and Kerry Hingston proudy stand in front of the restored LB80 at Kerry's sixtieth birthday party.
Slide-2: The old LB80 in its hey-day hauling the single deck trailer.
Slide-3: The boys lifting the cabin off the chassis during the restoration.
Slide-4: Transporting the cabin to the paint shop for the full bare-metal respray.
Slide-5: Painting the chassis in the workshop.
Slide-6: The cabin rubbed back to bare metal ready for the respray.
Slide-7: Looking like new after many months and hundreds of man hours.

Scania: Trucking in Australia

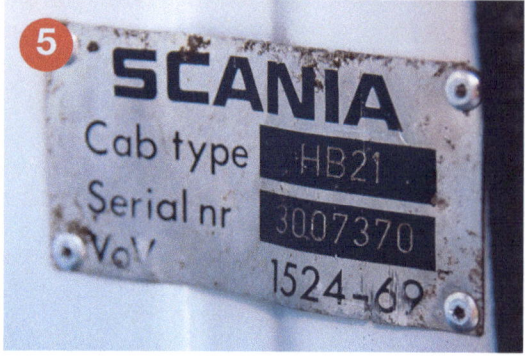

popularity, and I've got to admit I did look at them. After all, price wise, there was no difference compared to the Scania LB80," Kerry recalled. "I've still got the old advert, a brand new 1418 with the OM346 direct-injection diesel boasting 180hp (134kW) for only $13,506 including tax. But the features of Scania LB80 really set this truck in a class of its own. At the time, it was a very advanced truck. The LB80 had a little more power than the Benz, too. It had 210 horsepower 30HP more than the Benz. In addition, it had a full synchromesh transmission and hydraulic tilting cabin, which made it a much easier vehicle to service."

There is no lack of theories about why local operators bought so many imported heavy trucks from Europe in those early days of Australian trucking. Because today many truck historians still argue that the Scania LB80 and LB110 did more to advance truck driving and operating standards than any other type before or since.

The LB80 had 210 horsepower 30HP more than the Benz.

Nevertheless, Kerry Hingston is one man who can shed some light on the why?

It was no big surprise when Kerry answered with a firm confirmation that reliability and good spare parts backup was the primary motivation for Scania in the first place. The remarkable service he enjoyed from making that initial decision to purchase the second-hand Scania LB80 was indeed justified over the years, along with a conviction that he would continue to buy the same in future.

"Back then, in the formative years of our business Laurie Kelly was the Scania dealer in Tasmania," Kerry recalled. "He did a terrific job. He really backed the Scania product and had a good range of spare parts in stock. Having that good backup service makes a difference when it comes to how we deliver reliable service to our customers."

"When I purchased the LB80 Scania, reliability was one of the key features I was looking for," Kerry explained. "Over the years, it proved to be a very reliable truck. In fact, we kept it registered until 1997, so 24 years of service is a pretty good run by anyone's measure."

"It had a top speed of 60 miles per hour," Kerry recalled. "And you knew you were doing it too," He added with a smile. "In its life, it clocked over 1,236,000 miles and had its engine rebuilt three times.

Photo-1: The LB80 had a hydraulic cabin jack as standard.
Photo-2: A sensational paint job on this LB80.
Photo-3: Polished brass airline fittings glisten in the sunlight.
Photo-4: The old tube type rims were sandblasted and repainted.
Photo-5: The cabin serial number.

The original power setting of the DS8 turbocharged engine was 210HP. However, Kerry had the power bumped up to 230HP along the way. The transmission is the original Scania GS760 10-speed synchromesh splitter box with a first gear ratio of 9.74:1. The single reduction spiral bevel rear axle had the 4.86:1 ratio option.

The braking system on the LB80 was indeed advanced for the time with a dual-circuit air-pressure system, separate circuits to the front and rear axles, and the fitment of spring brakes at both axles to meet secondary and parking brake requirements. Brake drum diameters are 41.27 cm (16.25-inch) in diameter, with 8.9cm (3.5-inch) shoes at the front axle and 7.8 cm (7-inch) at the rear.

For truck enthusiasts who appreciate the nomenclature of truck models, the 'L' indicated Lastbil, which indicated a truck, and 'B' indicated Bulldog, which designated it was cab-over-engine (COE). The '8' signified the cylinder displacement of 8 litres, and '0' was the first model in the series.

"When the boys were doing the restoration, I was adamant that they did not put a turntable back on the old Scania; otherwise, Kerry would start using it for work again," Louise divulged. "I'd spent enough time travelling in that old truck when we were courting. The only way I'd get to see him back then was to ride in the old Scania," Louise added.

"It certainly was a very comfortable truck to ride in. But, truth be told, I'd often fall asleep in the cabin on the trips. So when the boys were coming to the end of the restoration and finalising the sign writing, I asked Brownie for a special request. Kevin Brown, from Spectrum Signs, is one of Tasmania's last remaining free-hand sign writers, so I enquired if he could paint the little 'Snoopy' character on the passenger side with his eyes shut because I was well known for falling asleep in it. But the caricature on Kerry's side has 'Snoopy' with his eyes open."

In the early days, Kerry found the fuel consumption of the Scania LB80 very favourable, along with the unit's reliability. Factors like these led Kerry to repeat the order for more Scania trucks as the company expanded, and recently, they took delivery of their 25th new Scania truck, a G480.

"I was certainly surprised when they drove the old LB80 in on the day," Kerry said. "Even our daughter Katie surprised me by flying home from Canada for the occasion and never letting anything slip about the truck. I'd always intended to restore the old LB80, but finding the time always proved challenging. Everyone involved did a magnificent job on the restoration, especially with all the detail, right down to the polished brass brake fittings. I certainly couldn't have done such a magnificent job on my own. However, I found out that my good friend Laurie Kelly, his son James and mate Ross did all the hard work on the restoration, so I'd really like to say a huge thanks to those guys for their terrific job."

"Sure, I have some fond memories of this old truck," Kerry added. "It was a damn robust, reliable machine that certainly made us a lot of money in its time."

Above: Louise and Kerry Hingston.
Top Right: Louise organised sign writer Kevin Brown to paint her Snoopy with the eyes shut because she often fell asleep when riding in the truck.
Middle: Kerry's Snoopy, on the other hand, has the eyes wide open.
Bottom: The registration label indicting the last year the old LB80 was registered as a working truck having toiled reliably for 24 years.

Reproduction Advertisement
First appeared in April 1978

SUPER
pure, potent power outstanding economy one stop back-up renowned comfort ... it's the Scania LKT 141!

SWEDE

Come rain. Come shine … new Scania LKT 141 is a great business proposition.

With 387 hp DIN of muscle developing maximum torque – 1480 NM (1092 lb.ft.) at just 1300 rpm you'll pull maximum payload with fuss free ease.

But new LKT 141's low stressed highway hauling power has a lot of other benefits too … reduced engine wear, tyre wear, fuel consumption, gear changes and engine noise. Not to mention one-stop back-up and service – because Scania is all Scania from bumper to bogey.

And just to make your job a little easier there's power steering, easy range change 10 speed transmission and a superbly comfortable Swedish safety cab complete with heated driving seat. In fact, new Scania LKT 141 is the perfect business partner – rain, hail or shine!

SCANIA
Saab-Scania Australia Pty. Ltd.

VIC.: Saab-Scania Aust. P/L, 202-210 Northbourne Rd., Somerton. 3062 Tel. 3054181 **NSW.:** Saab-Scania Aust. P/L, 66 Gordon Rd., Moorebank. 2170 Tel. 7278188. Saab-Scania Aust. P/L, 379 Edwards Stree West, Wagga Wagga. 2650 Tel. (069)251627. **QLD.:** Saab-Scania Aust. P/L, 53-55 Melbourne St., Rocklea, 4106 Tel. 3922919. **S.A.:** Diesel Motors, 288 Glen Osmond Rd., Fullarton Estate, 5063 Tel. 791678. **W.A.:** Saab-Scania Aust. P/L, 493-495 Great Eastern Highway, Redcliffe, 6104 Tel. 2777444. **N.T.:** Bridge Auto Sales, 14 Stuart Hwy., Darwin., 5790 Tel. 819003. **TAS.:** Garth Heywood Trucks, 6 Nairana St., Invermay, 7250 Tel. 316902.

A very early example of one of the Scanias on which the company established its reputation in Australia has been restored to its former glory.

A 1976 L111 bonneted Scania 4x2 was painstakingly brought back to life thanks to some dedicated effort by Scania's parts team and local truck restorers. The truck has been repainted in its original colour scheme, as specified by its first owner, Bill Larsen, who used it for logging in the foothills of the Great Dividing Range, around Mount Bogong and Lightning Creek.

"I liked the style of the truck. That's what drew me to it first," Bill admitted. "Scania appealed to me with its European looks, and also it had cross-diff locks, which were essential for the terrain I had to drive through.

"It was very manoeuvrable, and the single-drive was good on tyres, which was important in the bush. The gearing was very well suited to the task, and it had excellent brakes. They were the 8-inch drums which were larger than many other brands had at the time. The springs were strong enough to take a heavy load, as well," Bill added.

It was often very muddy on the logging routes in those days. The L111 was not Bill's first Scania, as he had previously owned a new L110. He later bought a stream of Scanias graduating to an early V8 142H, using them all in his logging transport business into the end of the 1980s.

"The Scania was good to drive, much better than American trucks. They also had a better steering lock, and they were much

Above Left: Bill Larsen with the restored Scania L111 he purchased in 1976.
Left: The L111 Scania now spends a more leisurely life style attending local truck shows.

> # Now that the L111 is restored, Scania exhibits it at a number of shows and field days each year.

quieter in the cab. It was unusual to see a Scania in the logging industry at the time," he revealed.

Scania enjoyed a strong reputation in the logging industry over many decades in Europe, as it does today. In northern Europe, Scania is a popular choice in the snow-covered logging routes that demand excellent grip, reliability and strength.

"I used the L111 in the softwood logging industry for ten years," Bill explained. "We switched to softwood when you couldn't access the hardwood forest anymore. So much of that area is National Park now. The truck was painted in Hamersley Brown and Caterpillar Yellow, and it had my name on the doors. For much of my career, I ran four to five trucks. After I traded the L111 I lost track of it. I recall someone saying it was painted red and blue," he says.

The truck was indeed painted in these colours when Scania acquired it in WA a few years ago.

The vehicle has been restored to a very high standard thanks to the care and devotion of Russell Lawrie, Scania Used Parts Manager at Campbellfield.

While the body needed some significant repair work and a full respray, the interior had survived in good condition and was largely retained, cleaned and tidied up.

"The truck had spent some time in Western Australia and was parked up there and allowed to deteriorate," says Allen Mounsey of Alrin Panels in Campbellfield, who repaired and resprayed the truck.

"We stripped off all the paint from the body, removed all the panels and left the superstructure. Next, we had to fabricate repair panels for the roof, the floor and the back of the cabin. Then we sprayed it with a filler primer and then finished it off in colours as close to the original as possible."

The truck had been restored once before so much of it was in good condition but some areas had rotted out.

"Mechanically, the truck was in good condition and had been fitted with a reconditioned motor sometime before, so we just tidied that up. Then, we rubbed the chassis back and painted it Hamersley Brown," Allen said.

"When the body was reassembled and painted, we called in our sign writer, Stuart Warren, who painted the livery and pinstripes by hand.

"The interior was fairly good all over with the roof-lining replaced at the previous restoration. The seat covers and door cards were repainted by our trimmer using a specialist paint for the vinyl facings," Allen said.

Alrin Panels has a long history of painting Scanias, though it usually paints new trucks for customers rather than bringing old trucks back to life.

Scania: Trucking in Australia

Diggin' It

It only takes a few minutes speaking to Allworks Excavations owner Robert Zolli to work out he's a straight shooter. He's been in the excavation game since he was 18, and now at the age of 62, the experience has made him a good commentator on the industry and people in general.

"My dad was a concreter and builder, so I got into the industry working with him," he revealed.

"I did an apprenticeship as a mechanic but had been working with my dad since I was a boy. The concreting eventually led to excavation machines and trucks. I've always been self-employed and in this line of work," Robert said.

He says the early 1970s were a different time when he started work. Back then, he adds, people were more honest, up-front and took responsibility on the worksite. But, while the times may have changed, these core values have remained with him and ultimately serve him well in business to the present day.

Interestingly, Allworks Excavations' no-nonsense approach has also transcended to the equipment they use, particularly its workhorse of choice: a 1991 Scania T 143 6x4 tipper. The T-series has been under Robert's ownership for over 17 years and has recently ticked over 1.5 million km.

Along with its work as a tipper, the truck often tows a trailer carrying excavation equipment; depending on the job, it could be anything from a skid-steer loader, traxcavator or one of two excavators, the biggest of which is a 9.5-tonne machine.

In a developed country such as Australia, rarely do you see a 23-year-old truck still earning its keep. Even more so, doing excavation work which can be brutal on equipment, but according to Robert, the old Scania doesn't miss a beat. It was a few years old when I got it, but I've had it for the majority of its life. There's nothing on it that doesn't work, and you can put it where you can't put a lot of other trucks., Robert said.

> **Rarely do you see a 23-year-old truck still earning its keep**

The trapezoidal suspension on the back is hefty – I've had it on 30-degree slopes moving dirt. You can't do that with an air-bag suspension. But, on the other hand, the truck's very stable. It's 11.5 tonnes, just the truck and tipper. Most of the newer stuff is 9 tonnes or a bit more, so you've got an extra 2.5 tonnes of stability.

Based in Tarrmbat, 24 km north of Melbourne, Allworks Excavations predominantly conducts residential excavations however has diversified over time to provide landscaping and concreting services.

"Nowadays, I do a lot of landscaping, especially shifting big rock; I go to Bonnie Doon quite often and pick up sandstone mudrock to build waterfalls. Sometimes I can squeeze in three

More than 20 years old, the T143 still regularly pulls an excavator on a trailer. A typical day involves moving a few loads of stone from the quarry to the yard or construction site. Robert says tipper work is 'the hardest you can do, but the T 143 shrugs it off.

Scania: Trucking in Australia

trips per day, covering 1200km in that truck carting rock. It's not uncommon to leave home at 4.00 am and get back between six or seven that evening after carting rock all day and tipping it off in places where a lot of trucks wouldn't go. So that's where I clock up the big milage," he declared.

Robert says that the rock carting is a task that his Scania takes in its stride and has more than enough power to handle a truck and trailer, often grossing 42-43-tonne and doing so effortlessly.

"The truck's got plenty of grunt, it came out standard with 450 horsepower, and it still pulls very well even today," he added.

Some might think an old truck is difficult to maintain and repair, but not Robert. As a trained mechanic, Robert does a lot of his own upkeep on the vehicle, and aside from general maintenance items, he says he had to invest little money in keeping it in top condition.

"Except replacing clutches and a gearbox, it's had nothing go wrong," Robert says.

"I've had the diffs out only to replace the O-rings on the diff locks, and that was only because when it was new, the line hauler never used the diff locks, so by the time I got it, the rings had gone hard.

"Scania certainly built trucks to last back then, there are no two ways about that, and importantly they designed them with repairability and ease of maintenance in mind. Thankfully they are easy to rebuild as well if needed."

"Tipper work is the hardest work you can do with them. We're on and off the road all the time, and putting them over trenches, it's a different ballgame. You've got to have a tough, sturdily constructed heavy-duty truck built to last in the rock-carrying business."

Top Left: Robert Zolli gives the thumbs up as he heads off to collect another load of decorative rocks.

Middle Left: The V8 sits low under the hood of the T143H.

Bottom Left: This Scania V8 produces 450 horsepower and pulls well says Robert.

Top Right: Robert Zolli's close-to-immaculate T143H V8 does not look like it has covered more than 1.5 million km.

Above Left: The steel tipper body and truck are very stable with a 11.5 tonne tare weight.

Above Right: Robert Zolli at the wheel of his Scania T143H

The **Multi-Leaf Trapezoidal Suspension**, with spring leaves of differing length, provides suspension and dampening through the internal friction between the leaves. This suspension is ideal for demanding operating conditions with heavy loads such as the conditions Robert operates his T143H. The high internal friction minimises the need for shock absorbers. It's robust economical and reliable as Robert can testify.

Scania: Trucking in Australia

SCANIA Truck Cabin Evolution

This timeline shows the evolution of the Scania, 'driver station' over seven decades. Scania is well known for its focus on comfort and safety for the driver, as highlighted by the thermos platform included in the 1950s design through the exceptional ergonomic modular infotainment centre in today's Scania.

1960s
A major change here is the flat wheel and instrument panel. But like in the 1950s, the buttons are small and unmarked; so you had to learn what they did, not rely on the symbols we use today. The seat has no suspension, and the steering column is non-adjustable, so long journeys could have been uncomfortable.

1980s
We are really seeing big changes here, especially with the introduction of the 3-series; that was when we first introduced the Scania sweep, the curved dashboard that we are famous for. There is a lot more luxury, too, with more supportive seats, adjustable steering column and lots more soft plastics.

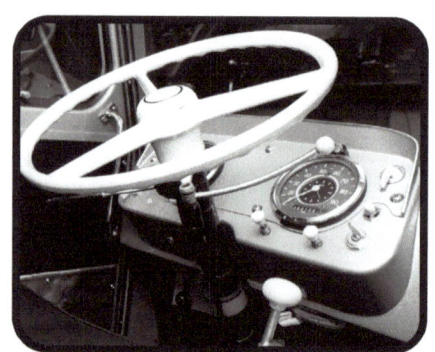

1950 — 1960 — 1970 — 1980

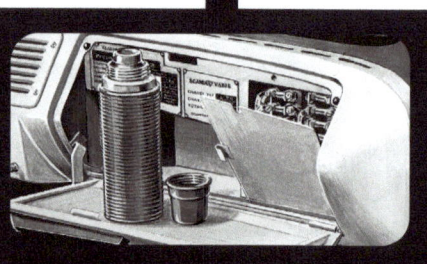

1950s
Beautiful but not very practical. The dash was mainly of a bright metal, which looks nice, but would have created quite a glare in sunny conditions. The dials are ringed with chrome; that's a classic touch, and something we use for inspiration today. And the steering wheel, although not comfortable for long journeys, is beautiful. The instrument panel is vertical, like today's trucks.

1970s
Longer and longer journeys meant that you can see the beginning of the driver comforts that we see today. The dash makes use of soft, black plastics for more of a luxury feel and some impact protection. The buttons are larger and use symbols to indicate their function. Centre consoles start making an appearance. These are great for storage for the driver, but not so good for allowing movement around the cab.

1990s
Like the 1980s, the sweeping, more vertical dash remains, making it easier and more comfortable to access the ever-growing range of function buttons. The dash and instruments are very clearly laid out and easily navigable. The centre console is still there, though, making backward and sideward movement difficult.

1990

2000s
The curved dash design panel affords the driver good vision of all instruments, and switches are within easy reach. All buttons and controls are ergonomically shaped. Based on transport application grouped together in a logical order The dash panel is designed on a modular system which is easy to adapt to the transport application.

2000

2020s
This is the ultimate in comfort. There's lots of textile and soft-touch plastic, which makes for a pleasant driving environment. Everything is clearly marked and many important functions are actually built into the steering wheel. The seats are like armchairs, with optimal adjustment, air suspension and integrated seatbelts for added comfort.

2020

Futuristic Dash Concept

Scania: Trucking in Australia

R560 PBS Double

Scania R560 heads the new high productivity PBS milk tanker B-Double that keeps Tasmanian operators ahead of the game with productivity gains.

Scania: Trucking in Australia

There's an upbeat camaraderie at Hingston Transport that you'd be hard-pressed to find in the depot of a stock-market-floated mega-fleet. The Scania R560 PBS B-Double operator Craig Bonde sums up the mood by telling us: "It's a bit like a bunch of mates working hard together."

"All the trucks have little motifs that reflect each driver's characteristics and passions," Craig explained. "The motif on this truck symbolises the night shift driver's love of football and his team North Melbourne along with his love of enjoying Boags Draught while he watches the footy. Then we have the dairy cow dressed in the football jersey for the milk we carry for Pura Milk hence the carton the cow is leaning on. These little things like that, which Kerry does, make us all feel part of a big family."

The Whitemore-based operation in the Meander Valley of Northern Tasmania isn't the sort of firm where huddled, hi-vis-wearing drivers who have an opinion on everything or complain endlessly about rumours generated by colleagues who know not (nor care not) what they're driving or why they're there.

"My men are all truck people; they're all dyed-in-the-wool truck enthusiasts," Owner Kerry Hingston informs us, "I have to say, rather proudly. I'm fortunate with every one of the men working here. It's a tightly-knit bunch of blokes who share a common interest in the job they do."

In fact, so positive is the mood, Kerry reckons it's also noticeable from the outside. "My men never have a problem, and the customers love' em!' he adds.

The business traces its roots back to Kerry's father, Viv, who carted livestock with a Desoto tray truck back in 1947. Yet European marques didn't enter the fleet until the early seventies when a young Kerry purchased a second-hand Scania log truck. So, impressed with the performance and reliability of that second-hand Scania LB80 along with the service they received from the local dealer that Scania trucks became the backbone of their operation.

The diversification and growth of their business into all areas of the agricultural industry, which incidentally takes them as far as Hobart in the south of the state, is attributed to the prompt and reliable service they provide their clients. But their willingness to push the boundaries of service and productivity through innovative transport solutions, such as the new Scania R560 and PBS B-Double trailers, does not go unnoticed.

Kerry admits he is content with growth from a one-truck owner-driver operation to where they are today, something about as big as you'd want to run on your own.

"The step up from here would be a corporate office with a transport operations desk and admin staff. That's not really what I'm about, so, on numbers alone, we're probably where we want to be, but you can never say never," he says.

The latest Scania combination in their fleet draws on the benefits of performance-based standards (PBS) to increase productivity and efficiencies not just for Hingston's but the dairy industry in Tasmania as well with the addition of high productivity B-Double.

Kerry Hingston had no hesitation specifying a Scania R560 to head up the new innovative PBS milk tanker B-Double. After all, Scania trucks have more than proven their reliability with the company for over four decades.

With the strict PBS criteria on the overall combination length and wheelbase dimensions, the ability of Scania to tailor a shorter wheelbase version of the R560 down from the standard 3553mm wheelbase to 2900mm made meeting the PBS requirements a simple process.

In addition, the 2 x 12-volt batteries are discreetly mounted at the rear of the R560 chassis to allow for greater fuel-carrying capacity. This gives the R560 plenty of driving range with a total capacity of 1030 litres of diesel fuel. There is a 710-litre fuel tank on the left-hand side of the chassis and a 320-litre fuel tank on the right-hand side next to a 75-litre Urea tank.

The compact dimensions of the R560 mean the combination enjoys unrestricted access with increased payload advantages. Moreover, Scania is one of the few manufacturers delivering a short wheelbase vehicle with high power outputs capable of comfortably pulling a fully loaded B-Double. That is partly thanks to the legendary 15.6-litre V8 under the cabin. Because the overall length of the V8 is much shorter than a traditional inline 6-cylinder engine, Scania can tighten up the wheelbase to suit unique applications such as PBS requirements.

Along with the unique features of the Scania, the Tieman Tankers are purpose-built to suit the application. In order to meet the PBS requirements, the rear axle on the tri-group is steerable, which significantly improves the combination's manoeuvrability on farm pickups and through the narrow suburban streets of Hobart.

> "The trailer steer axle automatically locks once the truck reachs 30kph."

The BPW axle is self-steering, which means that driver Craig Bonde doesn't need to do anything to make the axle steer. Instead, he just drives the Scania as he usually would.

Because the axle is self-steering when I turn it into a corner, the trailer follows the prime-mover more naturally," Craig explained. "It will steer itself according to the road, load and cornering forces being encountered. So now we have gone from a rather widespread footprint of a traditional tri-axle group to a far smaller tandem group with the steer axle at the rear. This design tends not to chop up the gravel hard stands in farms or driveways."

Scania: Trucking in Australia

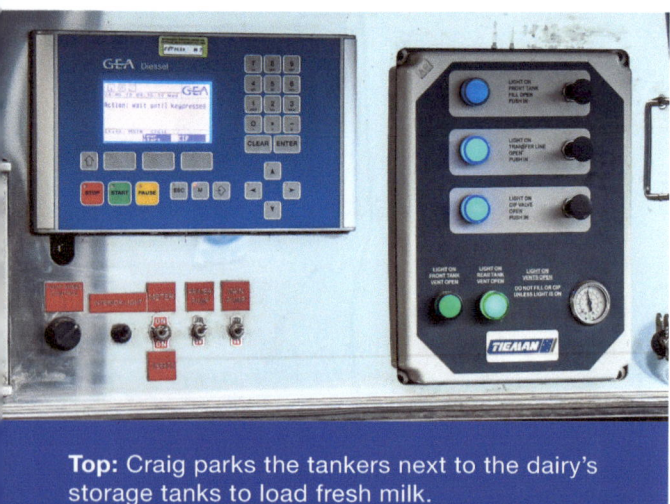

Top: Craig parks the tankers next to the dairy's storage tanks to load fresh milk.

Above: The lead tanker's pumping system is equipped with a state-of-the-art onboard computer tracking and printout system.

Below: Craig, collects a printed docket from the trailer with the number of litres collected off the dairy once the pump is switched off.

"The self-steering axle is self-centring too, which means it's straight-line towing is similar to a traditional tri-axle trailer," Craig explained. "The steer axle is automatically locked once they reach 30kph, and the lock releases once the road speed falls under 25kph. Reversing the unit is also quite simple, the same as reversing a traditional B-double. Because there is a solenoid fitted to lock the axle in the straight-ahead position when the unit is put in reverse," Craig adds. "As an additional measure, there is a manual override switch so I can manually lock the axle in the straight-ahead position if conditions are extremely slippery, such as when it's snowing."

Like the Scania R560, the Tieman milk tanker B-Double boasts some high-tech features, including a revolutionary pumping package and the inclusion of the BPW Trailer Electronic Braking System, which offers the Roll Stability Program that talks to the Scania R560 safety systems.

The Tieman pumping packing and hydraulic hose reel can be remotely moved to either side of the truck, making life far more manageable for drivers when the entrance to some milking vats demands such access flexibility. In addition, as the pumping gear has now been placed further forward on the tanker, Tieman has improved their pumping equipment's flow rate vastly.

Craig Bonde has the enviable task of piloting the Scania R560 and reckons when he first started driving an older Scania R560 a few years ago, he felt a bit guilty getting paid to drive it because of how easy and comfortable it is to operate.

Craig has lived in northwest Tasmania all his life and has been picking up milk for the past decade and a half.

Craig cites the smooth, comfortable ride in the cabin, the power of the Scania, and its road handling as some of the best attributes from a driver's point of view. He also adds that the extended service intervals mean he spends more time on the road than the drivers in other marques doing similar haulage tasks.

"The visibility out of this Scania is terrific," Craig explained. "The air suspension is smooth too, and the way the cabin is sprung means, I don't get any nasty jolts. It is a truly remarkable ride."

Another aspect that Craig pointed out was the spacious interior with ample storage space. Furthermore, under the bunk, 600 litres of storage capacity can be accessed through the passenger's side door locker.

"The more time I'm behind the wheel, the more money I earn, and when you're trying to save for a house, that's really important," Craig added. "It (the Scania R560) is excellent on fuel too. You notice it when you're pulled up next to other trucks at the fuel bowser, and you've all been doing the same job."

Like many in the industry, Kerry says that keeping afloat has to be the number one priority and adds that moving forward with the times and new technology is the key to keeping ahead of the game and delivering economic gains to customers.

"Our drivers are the most important part of our operation," Kerry added. "Without their skills and dedication, we wouldn't be where we are today. Providing them with a safe and comfortable vehicle like the Scania truck just makes their daily life a little easier out on the job."

"Over the years, Scania has worked with us to deliver solutions to our innovative transport concepts," Kerry explained. "The addition of the new R560 PBS B-Double is another example of how Scania's trucks have added productivity to our operation."

Top: All the main controls are at Craig's finger tips and the large information screen on the dash is easy to read at a glance.

Above: The remote-controlled hose enables loading from either side of the truck.

Below: The steering axle automatically unlocks when the speed drops below 25kph.

Scania: Trucking in Australia

GENERAL ACCESS

The roads might be narrow, windy and steep, traversing picture postcard scenery. Yet nestled along these hillsides of Northern Tasmania is a thriving agricultural industry, and it's here that local carrier Hingston Transport runs an impressive fleet of Scania trucks.

Digital phones do not enjoy good service in Tasmania, which makes receiving directions somewhat of a challenge at the best of times, especially when you're heading into some wild, uncharted country. "It's easy to find", came the garbled voice of Nicholas Hingston over the digital phone. "Jus` head to'ards St Helens, then follow your nose into town …" The signal now getting better towards the end of the message and the instructions slowly became more legible. "There's a parking area on the left-hand side of the road on the outskirts of town. I'll meet you there."

By mid-morning, the drizzling rain had settled in as I wound my way down the mountain to the east coast town of St Helens, famous for its big game fishing. Sure enough, just as Nicholas had predicted, the parking bay was up ahead. He had arrived a few minutes earlier and was filling out some paperwork on the steering wheel.

Like their grandfather and father before them, Nicholas Hingston and his brother Marcus are livestock carriers. Understandably the business has grown considerably in six decades to include the haulage of milk and general transport services to the agriculture industry.

The diversification and growth of their business into all areas of the agricultural industry is something the boys attribute to the prompt and reliable service they provide their clients, which incidentally takes them as far as Hobart in the south of the state. Along with a diverse range of trailers, the fleet consists of nine trucks ranging from a P-Series Scania to the R-Series B-Double units.

"We use the P-Series predominantly for our bulk milk haulage operation", Nicholas revealed. "They run 24 hours, seven days a week. Dad mostly does day shift in it alternating with one of our other drivers."

"A 620 HP engine powers the older white R-Series, which is a few years old now, and it has been an excellent truck," Nicholas explained. "My truck is the later R-Series with the newer 560 HP engine. Because the later specced engines have greater torque, we chose the 560 HP mostly to save on fuel, and the 560HP is returning very pleasing results in both performance and economy."

"One standout feature with this R560 is we specified a short wheelbase so we can get this B-Double down to 21-meters in length, allowing us general access," Nicholas explained. "That's why the polished alloy bumper is flush with the bodywork as every millimetre was critical getting the combination to fit."

We've stuck with the manual transmissions on our trucks," Nicholas said. "We feel they better suit our application and only employ skilled drivers. The manual transmissions in the Scanias are extremely robust, and we've not had any problems with them.

Above Left: The sheep jump excitedly through the gate on the way to the paddock
Above Middle: Sheep bustle through the yards on their way to greener pastures
Above Right: Nicholas' sheep dog wisely decided to stay out of the rain, preferring to watch the goings on from the comfort of his mobile kennel.
Below: Nicholas guides the R560 steadily along the winding undulating country road, all the while hoping the torrential rain will ease by the time he arrives at the farm to unload the sheep.

"Good working dogs are a stockman's greatest asset and will prevent stock from moving away from the stockman. This natural instinct is crucial when mustering stock in isolated gorge country, where a good dog will silently move ahead of the stockman and block up the stock until the rider appears. They will drive a mob of livestock for long distances in extremes of climates and conditions. They ride along in kennels built into the trailer chassis."

"Driver comfort in the Scania is car like," Driver John Townsend said. "I love the power of the V8 particularly in the hilly country we have here," he added.

"Look they're just so easy to drive. The vision out of them is terrific especially on a day like today when the rain is bucketing down and fog rolling in on these narrow roads. They are simply so easy to manoeuvre back into the stockyards. Really there is nothing bad to say about our Scania trucks John explained.

When you compare our typical operation where we operate comparatively low kilometre runs, mainly in rural environments. There are only two cities of any real size here in Tasmania; For us, there is little advantage in investing the additional money in an automated transmission system primarily designed to aid a driver in heavy traffic better. We feel that while it's not often published, auto boxes merely compensate for lack of driver skills."

"The Scania engines are well suited to our environment here in Tasmania," Nicholas informed. "But in order to achieve good economy, you need to be able to get the truck to cruising speed as quickly as possible, and these Scania engines are very good at achieving this. In addition, because the terrain in Tasmania is very undulating, we require ample torque across a broad range of revs, which makes maintaining cruising speed a lot easier on the truck with minimal gear changes.

"Torque in my truck peaks from around 1000 revs and remains usefully high all the way to 1400 revs," Nicholas explained.

Another feature of my truck is the rev counter with a dynamic green economy band. This feature is handy in our operation because when another driver gets in it, the truck is virtually telling them where it should be to deliver the best performance and economy."

Additionally, Nicholas has high praise for is the Scania retarder and downhill speed controller.

"With the retarder, it can be used manually by the driver to control the speed of the truck, or it can also be set to operate automatically, according to the requirements at the time," Nicholas explained. "For example, in the fully automatic mode, you simply make a quick dab on the brake pedal, which engages 'downhill speed control'. This means that the exhaust brake is operated automatically whenever needed, in conjunction with the retarder, to control the vehicle's speed.

"Alternatively, you can use the retarder manually simply by moving the retarder wand into the position you require. There are five positions, from mild through to maximum. The operator's guide tells you that using the retarder in the fully automatic mode will reduce wear on tyres and preserve the wheel brakes in a cool, fresh condition for when they are really needed."

Top: Marcus Hingston with one of the family's Scania trucks.

Middle: Nicholas Hingston looks backwards as he reverses his trailers on the stockyard ramp.

Bottom: Nicholas Hingston likes the room, comfort and vision from the Scania cabin.

"To give you an example of how we typically use the retarder," Nicholas added. "Take a traditional country road with bends and few undulations. In this instance, I would use the retarder manually just to reduce the truck overrunning on the short descents and occasionally to shed a few revs heading into the sharper bends. On the other hand, when I'm coming down the Sideling Range heading into Scottsdale, which is approximately a seven-kilometre descent, I use the retarder in automatic mode, which means the downhill speed is controlled entirely by the truck. This means I am descending the hill at a safe speed, yet still maintaining an efficient trip time, with minimal wear on the truck's service braking system."

"Another great advantage of Scania's retarder is that it does its braking through the transmission, which means you can down change a gear with it still engaged, and the vehicle's road speed does not increase during the gear change. It is so effective that I can virtually bring the truck to a complete stop by using the retarder and down-changing and not have to touch the truck's service brakes," Nicholas added.

By the time Nicholas arrived at the stockyards, the wind and rain had intensified, and the ground had turned to slushy mud. Maintaining traction in these conditions with the Scania is easy enough. Nicholas engages all the axle cross locks with the flick of a switch which gives positive drive to all four driving wheels.

"Our service can only be as good as the tools we use," Nicholas emphasised. "With Scania, we have an excellent product that is not only reliable but efficient to run, and they back up support we have from Scania first class.

"When you're on a good thing, you might as well stick with it," Nicholas concludes.

Top Left: Two of Hingston's Scania livestock trucks on the Northeast coast of Tasmania.
Top Right: Nicholas crosses the rising ford on the way to the farm.
Middle: Nicholas heading south out of the fishing town of St Helens on Tasmania's Northeast.
Below: Nicholas crossing the ford before the rising water cover the road.
Opposite Page: Approaching the narrow river crossing.

TRUCK SPECIFICATIONS

Model:	Scania R560
Engine:	Scania DC16 560 16-Litre V8
Horsepower:	560 hp (412)kw @1800 RPM
Torque:	1991lb/ft (2700Nm) @ 1000-1400 RPM
Gearbox:	Scania GRS0905R 14-speed Overdrive
Retarder:	Scania R4100D
Front Axle:	Scania AM 740
Front Suspension:	3 x 29 Parabollic 7500kg with anti roll bar
Rear Axles:	Scania Rb662/R660 with DCDL to both axles.
Rear Axle Ratio:	3.42:1
Rear Suspension:	Scania 4-Bag, 19.T
Brakes:	Scania electronically controlled disc brakes
Safety:	EBS with integrated ABS and traction control
Wheelbase:	3775 mm
Interior:	Velour Trim
Seats:	Premium driver's seat with armrests
Bumper:	Low mounted FUP
Battery Box:	24V Mounted rear of chassis

Scania: Trucking in Australia

Precision Agriculture with
All Wheel Drive XT

It's somewhat uncanny that for all the technology coming into trucking today, the trucks themselves still lead hard lives and need to be built tough.

And, no one knows this more than Tim Murfett, Manager of Launceston based Altrac Spreading. After all, his trucks have it harder than most specialised machines destined for heavy-haul and other severe service applications.

Left: Dirk Van-Namen (left), Tim Murfett, (right).
Below: The Scania 6x6 G440 is at home in the sheep paddocks on Northern Tasmania.

Scania's new XT construction models are a perfect example of the trend to blend cutting-edge tech with tough. It's a model range that leverages all of Scania's latest technologies, such as advanced telematics with an incredibly robust frame, high-horsepower diesel engines, and ground-gripping all-wheel-drive axle options.

That intricate blend of brain and brawn in the truck first attracted Tim to Scania.

"Today, we need a smart truck," Tim Murfett began. "Because the new generation of farmers who engage our services want accurate data on the amount of product we spread and where its spread. At the other end of the scale, we also need reliable and robust trucks to endure the rugged chassis twisting conditions we have in Northern Tasmania."

"We've increasingly become a key partner in our client's precision agriculture process," Tim added.

"When my father-in-law Dirk Van-Namen took over Altrac Spreading back in 2012, the technology in spreading equipment was considerably limited compared to the results we can deliver today," Tim explained. "I was new to the agriculture industry but came from a mechanical and transport background. So for the first 12 months, I juggled truck scheduling and driving one of our spreading trucks before permanently taking over the Manager's position. Mind you, Dirk and I jump into a spreader whenever we get the chance."

"I did a lot of logging back in my early days," Dirk said. "We even had a few Scania's on the logs back then, and they were good trucks," he added.

Today Altrac Spreading has diversified its services from spreading and transport to include crop and pasture sowing as well as filling in centre pivot irrigator ruts.

Along their expansion route, the path to increase productivity is one well-trodden by Tim and Dirk, chasing efficiencies where ever they can. It's a path that led them to their first 6x6 Scania, a G440 and subsequently to the P450 XT.

"At the time, we were searching for a vehicle that could carry more product to give us efficiencies through economies of scale and far more reliability than we were getting out of some

of the other marques in our fleet. Frankly, some of them weren't man enough for the job," he explained. "For instance, when we are on some of the larger farms, there can be a five or six-kilometre lead from the stockpile site to the paddock, which means that there can be a 20-minute loss of production from the time the truck leaves paddock, travels to the stockpile to load product and return to the paddock. That's primarily one reason the 6x6 Scania appealed to us."

"The other reason is the Scania is a very intuitive truck with a host of technical features that can link in with our unique body, which enable us more accuracy when spreading," Tim continued. "Most of the new generation of farmers have a college education and really know their production costs and monitor their soils to enhance crop growth to maximise their yields. It's what's known today as precision agriculture."

Simply put, precision agriculture is a farm management approach primarily based on technology and data collection. Farmers use anything from drones, GPS, and sensors to soil sampling and variable rate applications to make agribusiness more accurate.

"Today, we work closely with our clients and based on their requirements; we can plot the path for spreading in the paddock and precisely measure and vary the amount of product we spread, then at the completion of the spreading process, provide the farmer with an accurate record of the amount of product spread in that paddock."

"There is a significant cost saving for the customer straight away," Tim revealed. "Now we can guarantee to minimise overlap passes which means no wasted fertiliser or seed and importantly waste fuel and time. In addition, with the variable rate application, the machine can dispense more product in areas of the paddock that require dense coverage and less where lighter coverage is required. This approach certainly provides the maximum benefit to the soil."

However, Tim admits that when he first looked at the 6x6 Scania, it certainly appeared to be a premium product on paper, a fact that was quickly confirmed when the quote for the vehicle came in $20K higher than his last spreader acquisition.

"Then there was a price jump from the G440 to the new P450 XT," Tim revealed. "At first glance, it might seem somewhat hard to quantify such a significant gap in the price from one vehicle to the other. However, for us, though, we had to look at what we were getting in that package.

Not only did we need to consider how the new technology will benefit our operation but also how the efficiencies of this new machine will reduce costs. Then it was a matter of weighing up the integrity of the product along with its backup support to ensure that we can provide the level of service we are promising our customers," Tim explained.

> "Today, we need a smart truck"

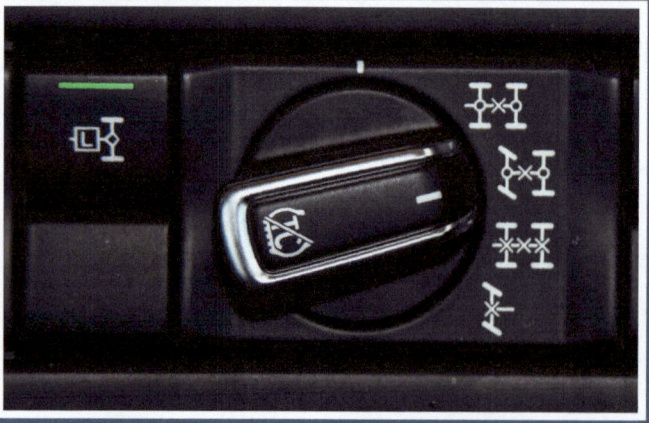

"Importantly, we had to assure ourselves that the additional price increase in equipment came with a significant productivity gain," Tim explained. "If our costs rose too high because of the investment in equipment and we're forced to pass this on, then farmers would start looking at purchasing tow-behind spreaders for their tractors to do their own spreading. It's that simple! Because farmers are always looking at ways to reduce their costs too. Thankfully when we started looking into the Scania trucks in-depth, it quickly became apparent they would deliver the efficiencies we were looking for."

Tim conceded that when he started crunching the numbers, he couldn't afford not to have the new Scania 6x6. The legal road-going payload increase from the smaller MAN 4x4 to the Scania 6x6 went from 4.5 tonnes to 7 tonnes (55.56 per cent), and in the paddocks even higher. The new larger Southern Spreaders bin spread pattern went from 34 meters to 50 meters (47 per cent). Because the Scania 6x6 carries far more fertiliser in the field, the number of trips that Scania trucks have to make back to the stockpile is reduced by 37.5 per cent.

"When you weighed the productivity and economic gains we were getting for a small 8.7 per cent increase in the purchase price, we just had to have the Scania," Tim said. "In fact, when I first saw it in the afternoon, I went back to my motel room and did the sums, then rang Dirk, and we both agreed that the Scania 6x6 was the way of the future. So, Dirk rang and ordered it that night."

Since the first 6x6 went into service in mid-2018, it quickly became apparent that Dirk and Tim had made the right choice. The larger 440 horsepower truck was carrying more fertiliser, towing a tag trailer with the loader, and burning approximately the same amount fuel than the smaller 4x4.

"Like all transport operations, fuel burn is one of the highest costs," Tim explained. "It did worry me how the Scania was going to go when it came to fuel, considering it had the larger engine and more power. But once it started working, the extra power proved to be a greater asset because it can get more product to the job site quicker and climb the hills at a reasonable pace."

"One thing we've had on all our spreader trucks is the central tyre inflation system which enables us to raise and lower the tyre pressure from inside the cabin on the fly. This feature, combined with the Michelin 495/70 R24 XM47 floatation tyres, is important when spreading in paddocks as soil compaction is a big concern for the farmers from the weight of our vehicles on their crops.

However, lowering the tyre pressure in the paddocks increases the surface area of the tyre's footprint over the ground and reduces the kgs/cm2 load on the ground. The added advantage is the greater the tyre footprint; the more traction improves, much the same as 4x4 enthusiasts lower their tyres when they're on the sand."

Above: Altrac's original G440 brought new efficiencies and productivity gains to the business which meant it wasn't long before an XT P450 joined the fleet.

Top Right: The touch screen provides the driver with a detailed live time view of the paddock and product spread rate.

2nd Right: Topcon positioning system steering wheel in the XT P450 guides the truck around the field.

3rd Right: The XT P450 retains the standard dash layout.

Bottom Right: This rotatory dial enables the driver to easily select cross-locks through to all-wheel-drive in an instant.

Below: Tim Murphett, loading fertiliser into the G440 as the XT P450 returns to the paddock with a fresh load.

"During a particularly wet week back in spring, the Scania 6x6 was spreading in a large paddock down Fingal way, it had been going in and out of the paddock several times, barely making a mark in the grass where it had been," Tim recalled. "One of our 4x4 spreading fertiliser nearby had some product left over. So we drove it into that same paddock. It went about five meters and sunk down to the axles. We couldn't believe how easy the bigger 6x6 was working in such wet boggy conditions and barely leaving any evidence it was there."

TRUCK SPECIFICATIONS

Model:	Scania G440 6x6	Scania P450 XT 6x6
Engine:	Scania DC13 440 13-Litre inline-6-Cylinder	Scania DC13 450 13-Litre inline-6-Cylinder
Horsepower:	440 hp (328)kw @1800 RPM	450 hp (335)kw @1900 RPM
Torque:	1696 lb/ft (2300Nm) @ 1000-1300 RPM	1733 lb/ft (2350Nm) @ 1000-1300 RPM
Gearbox:	Scania GRS905R 14-speed Direct	Scania GRS905R 14-speed Direct
Gearbox shift:	Opticruise	Opticruise
Transfer Case:	GT900	GT900
Retarder:	Scania R3500	Scania R4100
Alternator:	Scania 24V 100amp	Scania 24V 100amp
Compressor:	Knorr 720CR, twin cylinder, 800 L/min with air dryer	Knorr 720CR, twin cylinder, 800 L/min with air dryer
PTO:	ED 120P	ED 120P
Air Cleaner:	High rear mount with pre-cleaner & safety filter	High rear mount with pre-cleaner & safety filter
Propeller Shaft:	All wheel drive P540	All wheel drive P540
Propeller Shaft:	Front P460	Front P460
Steering Box:	TAS 85 18.6:1	ZF 8098 22.2-26.2:1
Front Axles:	Scania AMD901	Scania AMD901TZP
Front Axle Ratio:	3.95:1	4.04:1
Front Suspension:	3 x 29 Parabolic	2 x 32 Parabolic
Rear Axles:	Scania AD1303P axle housings with RBP 735 gears	Scania AD1303P axle housings with RBP 735 gears
Rear Axle Ratio:	3.93:1 with diff locks to both axles	4.041 with diff locks to both axles
Hub Reduction Ratio:	3.81:1	3.65:1
Rear Suspension:	Scania 4-Leaf Parabolic, with roll bar	Scania 4-Leaf Parabolic, with roll bar
Brakes:	Electronically controlled drum brakes with auto slacks	Electronically controlled drum brakes with auto slacks
Tyres:	Michelin 495/70 R24 XM47	Michelin 495/70 R24 XM47
Safety:	EBS with integrated ABS and traction control	EBS with integrated ABS and traction control
Wheelbase:	3850mm	3850mm
Cab Tilt:	Mechanical	Electronic
Interior:	Vinyl & Textile Trim	Vinyl & Textile Trim
Seats:	Premium driver's seat with armrests	Premium driver's seat with armrests
Bumper:	Powder coated double tube steel	Powder coated double tube steel
Battery Box:	2x12V, 180 amp Chassis mount LH side	2x12V, 180 amp Chassis mount LH side
Fuel Tank:	1 x 300L R/H side	1 x 500L R/H side
Adblue tank:	1 x 50L R/H side	1 x 47L R/H side

Left: The spray pattern of these spreader bins on the back of these Scania trucks is 50 meters.
Below: The P450 XT 6x6 is equipped with central tyre inflation.
Middle: The Scania trucks line up to load fertilizer at the stockpile.
Bottom: The P450 XT 6x6 charging moves swiftly around the paddock when spreading.

Take a look at the steering wheel in these Scania trucks; it is quickly apparent that they're a little more sophisticated than standard. They're equipped with the Topcon electric self-steering that enables the truck to steer itself in the paddock to pre-plotted courses to ensure the product spread is directed where it has been programmed. But, of course, the driver can still override the system at any time simply by turning the wheel to avoid an object in the path. "It's all part of our precision agriculture program," Tim added.

The trucks still retain all their original functions for the on-highway side of the operation.

Scania's DC13 engine powers the latest Scania 450 XT, which drives through the GRS905R 14-speed direct transmission with Opticruise shift into the GT900 transfer case. The transfer case directs power to the forward and rear axles according to the conditions. In addition, this vehicle features the R4100 Retarder, which does an excellent job in the hilly country around Tasmania.

When asked how happy he was with the two Scania 6x6 spreader trucks, Tim answered, we're that impressed with our Scania trucks and they're doing such a great job we've actually ordered two more 4x4, which will arrive in the next month or so and scheduled another 6x6 in time for next season.

Scania: Trucking in Australia

A LONG HAUL
to the Top

The GFC prompted Gladstone-based Waterson Diesel owners Darren and Sherrin Waterson to switch from vehicle servicing to long-haul transport. However, Scania's reliability and performance mean they haven't looked back.

The reliability and strength of Scania trucks are at the forefront of a Queensland company's successful transformation into an award-winning specialised transport business forged in the wake of the Global Financial Crisis. Nowadays, based on a sprawling 1,000-acre property on the outskirts of Gladstone's busy industrial and port city, about 550 km north of Brisbane, Waterson Diesel was formed in 1999 by husband and wife team Darren and Sherrin Waterson.

Founded on Darren's trade as a diesel mechanic, Waterson Diesel initially specialised in providing diesel fitting, maintenance and repair services to several of the city's major entities, including Rio Tinto and Transpacific.

Darren's family history in the Gladstone district stretches back five generations, and for the first ten years of operation, business was good for Waterson Diesel. Fatefully and fortunately, the couple had also seen an opportunity to diversify into providing transport and machinery services to several clients. Their first truck was a used Scania P114 eight-wheeler with a hook lift body, bought in 2005 for collecting and delivering heavy-duty skip bins.

"That was an excellent truck," Darren says emphatically. "We had an excellent run. It just never let us down."

Yet it wasn't just the reliability and efficiency of their first Scania that instilled a lasting impression on Darren and Sherrin Waterson. Scania's service and support structure, specifically through the Richlands dealership in Brisbane, was a significant attribute that would ultimately play an influential part in forging an even stronger relationship between Scania and Waterson Diesel.

However, the fierce impact of the Global Financial Crisis had a truly life-changing effect on the future direction of Waterson

Diesel. As Darren explained, "The GFC quickly led to a significant reduction in maintenance spending by a couple of the big companies we worked for. Consequently, our diesel fitting work dried up in a big hurry.

"But the truck and machinery sides of the business were going well. Consequently, by 2009, we faced a relatively simple decision."

Obviously enough, that decision was to forego the diminished diesel fitting business and concentrate on expanding a transport enterprise specialising in the movement of equipment and heavy machinery, as well as hiring various types of earthmoving equipment.

"It was time to move on. Definitely time!" says a resolute Sherrin Waterson.

At the core of the company's new business platform was the determination to offer well-presented, high-quality trucks and an extensive range of trailing equipment catering at short notice to a wide assortment of loads. Some of the diverse Waterson loads include mobile generators and small loaders, portable huts and containers, large excavators, dump trucks, water tankers, cranes and bulldozers.

On the decision to keep the existing company name rather than change to a more transport-centric title, Darren explains simply, "The Waterson Diesel name and even the colour of the equipment were already well established in Gladstone. So it was just a matter of choosing a new logo that reflected the type of work we were now doing."

After dabbling in a few second-hand trucks to meet immediate needs, it wasn't long before Darren's regard for the Scania product led to the delivery of their first new truck. Darren specifically chose an R500 V8 prime mover to haul a quad-axle heavy haulage float.

Building on the experience of their first Scania, Darren concedes the R500 played a critical part in establishing Waterson Diesel's enviable reputation for professional service with a broad customer base in and around the Gladstone district.

Scania has, in fact, been the only brand of new heavy-duty truck bought by the company, with the initial R500 joined by a G440 eight-wheeler tilt tray rigid in 2011, Two G440 prime movers and another R500 in 2012, and an R620 V8 flagship arriving late last year.

"I've always liked Scania, and it was a conscious decision to run one brand of truck," he candidly explained. "To me, Scania represents good value-for-money, but it's also appealing in a lot of different ways, including appearance, which is a significant factor in customer considerations.

"There are certainly no regrets about the decision to go with Scania," he says earnestly before citing reliability, performance, fuel efficiency, ride quality, low noise and driver ease as inherent features of the company's various Scania models.

All Waterson Scanias are equipped with the Opticruise automated transmission, multi-stage retarder, and exhaust brake.
Importantly, Darren quickly reaffirms that Scania's response to any service issues is "exceptionally good."

The successful transformation of Waterson Diesel from a diesel fitting business to a professional, well presented transport operation saw the company last year awarded first place in the industry category of Gladstone's 'Observer Westpac Best in Business Awards.'

"Waterson Diesel runs only high-quality equipment providing a consistent service, and maintains an experienced and professional team of employees," a proud Darren Waterson said at the awards ceremony.

Scania, of course, is equally proud to be a vital contributor to the success of this impressive family business.

PRETTY IN PINK

Nowadays, it's not a particularly rare occurrence to find a female behind the wheel of a heavy-duty truck. What is not so common, however, is to find a woman at the wheel of a heavy-duty truck hauling a high, wide and heavy piece of machinery, such as the loads regularly hauled by Waterson Diesel.

Yet that's precisely the job description for Kayla Carter, an attractive '30 something' originally from South Australia who doesn't hesitate to acknowledge the willingness of Waterson Diesel to provide both the opportunity and the training for a job normally considered a man's domain.

With a diverse background that includes a commercial coxswain licence gained in South Australia's aquaculture industry, Kayla explains that a move to Queensland started a chain of events that now sees her steering a Scania G440 prime mover hauling a mix of low loader and flat-top trailers.

"I'm certainly still learning, and learning something new nearly every day," she says thoughtfully, "Thankfully, I'm given opportunities here that I probably wouldn't get anywhere else. In the 18 months, I've been here, I've come to love the job, the people, the company, the equipment."

On the Scanias, there are no complaints whatsoever. "Vision and the ease and comfort of the truck definitely make the job easier," she remarks. "Manoeuvrability is a big asset, so too is the flexibility of the (Opticruise) transmission, especially when you're working in tight spaces around town."

But about that pink Scania badge, and even pink tank straps and a pink hard hat?

"I suppose there are some concessions to being a female," she laughs. "Still, I'm not saying I don't like it. On the contrary, it's a nice touch .... for a woman!"

As for hiring a woman to do what some would view as strictly a man's domain, Darren Waterson responds simply, "Kayla does the job, does what she's asked, she's quick to learn and takes good care of the equipment. Where's the problem?"
Absolutely!

R730 IN THE HARDWOOD

When George Catalano needed a new logging truck, he took a tip from neighbour Matt Winterfield and switched from American iron to Swedish steel, and he hasn't looked back.

The forests around Mount Gambier in South Australia's eastern corner through to Portland in Victora are lush with renewable trees and known as the 'Green Triangle'. They grow fast, and they grow thick, and then, like arable crops, they're harvested and sent for processing. Transporting mill logs or chipped wood products keeps many operators busy through biting cold and stinging rain or sweltering heat. Forest roads are often gnarly, pot-holed, washed out or just plain slippery. Hence, traction and plenty of it is a crucial ingredient for successfully hauling a fully-laden 68.5-tonne combination out of the woods, onto the highway and off to the chipper, port or mill.

Not surprisingly, George Catalano's father was a logging contractor. So the lure of the wide-open highway was more of a natural progression for George, but what has shocked him has been the ease with which a lifetime's devotion to American-built trucks has evaporated after such a short association with Sweden's finest: a Scania R 730 V8.

Undoubtedly the 16.4-litre Scania flagship provides an irresistible lure to owner operators seeking reward for those hard years battling for survival. But George doesn't keep his new R 730 to himself. Instead, the truck is double shifted, with him sharing the driving with his long-time friend, Leigh Stevenson.

The Go-cat Transport business commenced interstate freight runs over nine years ago before winning a lucrative log haulage contract from the bush to sawmills and ports four years back.
Mount Gambier-based heavy haulage operator Matt Winterfield bought an R 730 for his float work. He passed this to his driver Peter O'Dea before securing a second identical truck to drive himself after Peter gave the European cab-over a big tick of approval. Matt was amazed at how quickly the intoxicating mix of power, smoothness and economy won him over, so he was not shy to pass on the good oil about the R 730 to his friend George.

the intoxicating mix of power, smoothness and economy won him over

"We have now had the R 730 on the road for eight months now, and it's clocked up 100,000 km, and it has performed awesomely well," George said, at the time of writing, about the eye-catching V8 with its bright blue and white paint scheme.

"There's been no trouble with it. It has been chugging along really well," George added with a grin.

"We're now double shifting it because the work is there, and we clocked up 30,000km last month," he said. "A typical haulage run for the R 730 is a 450-500 km trip, and we can do up to three trips a day, depending on where we go. We either work in South Australia or Western Victoria, mostly carting blue gum timber and occasionally some pine.

"We cart for Merrett Logging," George said, "they have looked after us well, kept us going, even in the quiet times. When fully loaded at 68.5-tonnes, we'll get around 1.6 – 1.7 km per litre.

Victoria has a lot of hilly terrain, and the truck works hard all day. It's ether 100 per cent throttle climbing then 100 per cent braking down the other side. There is no in-between. Yet compared to the American truck we had, the Scania is

doing far better trip times and is far better on fuel. We used to get only 1.3 – 1.4 km/l," George said. "Fuel-wise, the R 730 has been remarkable.

"If we ran in South Australia only, where its far flatter, we would see better figures, but 1.7 km/l overall is excellent considering the conditions we have to operate in. We're also running it for five years on the Scania repair and maintenance contract.

"We'll double shift this R 730 on logs till mid-way through its five-year plan and then run it on another less demanding logging contract for the remainder of the time. But I specified it with a sleeper so we could do interstate work with it if required. Certainly, the sleeper cab will be an advantage when we sell it. I reckon it's the first Scania R 730 in this area doing logs.

"I'm sold on Scania now, and we won't buy anything else. What sold me on the truck was the quality of the driver comfort and things like the wiring looms, engine bay, and the insulation of the cab.

"You can't beat the comfort of the R 730, and it just flies up hills smooth as silk. We see reduced travel time because of the additional uphill speed, around 20 km/h faster than the old American truck. So you're not worried about logbook hours anymore.

"This is the first Scania Leigh has driven, and he is ecstatic about it," George added. "He absolutely loves it, and in fact, because we have the R 730 for the photos today, he had to drive a spare American truck, and he is ticked off," George said with a laugh.

"I worked with Paul Riddell at Scania Wingfield in Adelaide to get the specification of this truck just right. I'd had plenty of

Above: George at the wheel, where he feels very comfortable. The truck can run up to three haul routes daily, clocking up well over 1500 km between the two drivers.
Above Left: According to George, fuel consumption has been impressive, saving a significant sum of money on every run thanks to the very frugal engine, despite its power and payload.
Opposite Page: Pulling out of the forests outside Mount Gambier requires negotiating some fairly average roads, so positive traction is vital at all times. The Scania delivers in spades.

experience specifying American trucks over the years, but Paul was a real help and suggested hub reduction diffs to protect the drivetrain and provide good traction.

"We opted for super-singles on the front, as per Paul's recommendation, and they have been brilliant. Drive tyre life after 100,000 km is good, they still look like new, and there would easily be another 70,000 – 80,000 km in them, and it wouldn't surprise me to get 200,000 km from them, even though this work includes 30 km each way on white metal, gravel and mud," George explained. "I wasn't sure how an auto transmission would go in the bush. Leigh said he's been driving through bad patches where others would not make it through. But overall, the traction is that good off-road.

"The ride quality is outstanding, especially off-road. Because it is so smooth, you might think it feels disconnected off-road, but you can still get plenty of that seat-of-the-pants feel, so you know exactly what it is doing on dirt, which impressed the hell out of me," George said. "Honestly, I didn't expect that.

"The Scania Retarder is an absolute bonus for us, especially in the hilly parts of Victoria. Leigh is amazed and

"The Scania Retarder is an absolute bonus for us"

says he can go 99 per cent of the day without touching the service brakes, which greatly reduces our running costs, but additionally, brake wear on the trailers also dropped dramatically."

George uses Scania service agents OGR in Mount Gambier as well as the Scania branch at Wingfield, Adelaide, for the maintenance of the R 730. He's also had a stint with the Scania Driver Trainers as part of the delivery process.

"I had some Scania driver training about 18 months ago, which was very good," George said. "It gave me a new perspective, and driving this truck is different. The Peak Efficiency programme was outstanding, and I loved learning how to drive the truck as efficiently as possible.

"Matt Winterfield and I are good mates, and we both have R 730 V8s, so we'll be comparing our scores on the driver support system. Leigh is also getting into it and figuring out how to get his scores up. Consequently, he said that having the scores on the dash in front of you and getting real-time tips on keeping the score up is very useful," George added.

> George plans to run the R 730 on logs for now but has specified that the truck can switch to running interstate freight if the logging work dries up.

The Good Fuel

Michelle and Grant Harris

Scania: Trucking in Australia

Trevor Bale, says 1.3-1.4 km per litre with 100,000 litres of fuel on and into a headwind is a good result.

Surprisingly the southeast corner of Western Australia is not heavily populated per square kilometre, yet significant volumes of traffic flow across the Nullarbor Plain daily. Esperance-based BP distributor, South East Petroleum, is located 200 km due south of the main east-west arterial. Owned and run by Grant and Michelle Harris, the business keeps the traffic moving by replenishing the highway roadhouses and truck stops as well as the region's small-town filling stations, using a fleet of modern, safe and stable Scania prime movers.

The distances between stops can be vast, so fuel deliveries must be reliable because there are no alternatives when crossing the desert between South Australia and the continent's western coastline.

One of the company's drivers, Glenn 'Bindi' Sievwright, undertakes South East Petroleum's longest delivery run weekly. It's a 2-day 1,500 km round trip to Cocklebiddy Roadhouse, carting 98,000 litres of fuel in a C-train formation. It's a run Bindi knows well, having undertaken it for 30 years. Week in, week out. So not surprisingly, he's something of a celebrity in the region. When he's not heading to or from Cocklebiddy, he is busy on day-long runs in more 'local' areas.

Grant Harris says the fuel distribution business is quite seasonal as agriculture is a big part of life in this part of the state. Fuel is in demand in the seeding season and later for the harvest, with farmers running all manner of farm machinery and, of course, fuelling the trucks transporting grain to storage facilities.

"For many years, much of our business focused on delivering fuel to local customers, but in recent times we have also created a market among the mining companies," Grant revealed. "The business has grown organically over the years, and we see this continuing.

"The mining industry is undergoing some rationalisation, despite new projects being on the horizon. But, the rural sector will continue to grow with cattle and sheep and grain farming. "Over the past 20 years, we have seen a huge expansion of grain farming which has increased the demand for fuel to run the machines quite considerably," Grant explained. "This is a very productive grain growing area, and the returns can be impressive if the weather plays along."

South East Petroleum owns six prime movers, all of which are Scanias. The modern fleet includes Scania R 620 V8s, tasked with pulling three tanker trailers with a combined 99,000 litres of fuel, 90 per cent of it typically diesel.

"We have six trucks and six drivers, and each sticks to his truck in everyday operations. We find this means they look after the truck and the cargo better. We tend not to double shift because many of our customers don't like or cannot take deliveries at night," Grant admitted. "We have cultivated a loyal and stable customer base, and they appreciate the service we deliver, and we pride ourselves on offering a competitive price.

"Having one brand of truck in the yard makes life easy if we need to switch prime movers between trailers. All the axle spacings are the same, so there are no loading/weight issues," says Trevor Bale, who is involved with operations and maintenance and is also a driver. "For dangerous goods transport, it's another layer of safety as well, as all the drivers know where all the controls are."

The fleet comprises an older P-series 360 hp prime mover and a newer 440 hp P-series used to deliver smaller loads to farms in the Esperance region. In addition, there are three R 620 V8 prime movers, a vehicle Trevor believes is ideally suited to fuel delivery work.

"In the last five years, we have invested considerable money to modernise our fleet, both in prime movers and trailers. We look to change the prime movers over every five years, and we are now seen to be a leader in dangerous goods and fuel transport.

"We'll cover around 500,000km on average over the period in each truck, but some of the smaller ones only travel 60,000km a year, but it is hard work down the gravel farm roads.

Mick Creedon, covers around 2500 km a week and been driving for South East Petroleum for 20 years.

"For C-trains pulling 80-tonnes at 120-tonnes gross, the R 620 makes for a stress-free drive," he says. "We're seeing 1.3- 1.4 km per litre with 100,000 litres on board, depending on the day and the headwinds," he said. "The fuel consumption of the Scania trucks is excellent. We keep track of our fuel use and are happy with what we achieve. The driving involves lots of time stationery – running the PTO to drive the hydraulics on farms off-loading."

Trevor has a long history with dangerous goods transport, having worked for a fuel company for 12 years. He started off driving for Esperance Freight Line's Michael Harding's father. Their fuel company purchased Scanias among a mix of vehicles. Still, Trevor was always impressed by the comfort and quietness of the Scania cab that reduced fatigue over a long shift.

"The layout is good for a driver, and you can stand up in the cab," he added. "The bunk is OK, and the Opticruise and Retarder are winners. The Retarder particularly gives the Scania driver an advantage because you just ease the wand on and never have to touch the service brakes. Safety is critical to Dangerous Goods drivers.

"We like the weigh scales on the axles because we must know how much load we have onboard, especially as we off-load several times during a shift.

"We have to manage the load to ensure the compartments remain balanced, so the vehicle remains stable on the road, and this also prevents damage to the surface. We run a lifting axle on the trailers to cut fuel consumption and reduce wear and our impact on the road surface. There can often be 100 km between off-loading points, so stability is important," Trevor informed.

"Every day when we plan the drops, we look at the orders to determine which drops we make first to ensure the load remains stable as it diminishes.

"Fully loaded with two barrels, we're carrying around 74,000 litres, and with three barrels, we're up around 99,000 litres.

"The Scania is very stable on the road even when half-loaded," Trevor said. "We run the new Scanias on the Maintenance and Repair programmes and service at 15,000 km intervals.

"The benefit to the business of having a set amount allocated for maintenance and repairs means we can accurately forecast how much we will be spending. We closely monitor the kilometres travelled and ensure the trucks get serviced on schedule. We check the trucks ourselves every fortnight, and the trailers get checked every 7000 km," Trevor added.

"We have built a good relationship with the Kewdale branch, and we will stick with them," Grant says. "For our operating conditions, a European truck suits our type of work. "Our local workshop, Kip & Steve's Mechanical Repairs in town, looks after routine maintenance for us," Grant explained. According to Scania WA's Michael Berti, the South East Petroleum experience is an excellent example of how Scania can deliver for the fuel distribution industry.

"Scania goes to a lot of trouble to design and manufacture fuel delivery prime movers that come from the factory with many features built-in to make Dangerous Goods transport safer and more efficient.

"This means there's less time spent converting the trucks when they arrive in Australia, and the DG-specific features are manufactured to a consistently high standard. "Scania understands fuel distributor needs, and we are very pleased to see South East Petroleum continuing to build its relationship with our company," he explained. "The distances they cover and the impressive fuel results they achieve underline just how well-suited Scania trucks are for this type of work.

"When you are travelling these distances in relatively unpopulated areas, reliability and durability are paramount," he says. "And driver comfort too plays an important role for DG transport. Scania has proven to be the perfect choice for this work."

Scania: Trucking in Australia

PUMPED UP
P380

Scania's NTG P380 is pumping more than just tiling screed to building and construction sites around the country. Their unique custom-made pump truck eliminates deadly silica dust and dramatically reduces production costs and time while enhancing safety in the workplace.

West Australian headquartered ScreedPro, a wholly Australian owned company, has been supplying commercial grade tiling screed to Australia's leading floor contractors and builders for over two decades. Over the years, they have refined their technology and systems to become the preferred supplier to virtually all major construction projects in Western Australia. In addition, they are rapidly expanding their services along the East Coast.

The introduction of their first new Scania P380 and custom-made trailer a few months ago radically transformed the floor screeding industry overnight. The success of this first unit cemented the future for a total of six new Scania P380 and trailer units scheduled to be on the road before Christmas, with a similar rollout schedule planned for later in the next year.

Before the arrival of the ScreedPro Scania P380 and trailer pumping unit, floor screed was traditionally mixed by hand and then wheelbarrowed into the building.

"There was a lot of manual handling with this process," NSW General Manager Les Stockdale explained. "To compound the problem, at high-rise job sites, we were always relying on materials hoists and other site infrastructure to get to these upper levels. It was extremely time-consuming and labour intensive. Then there was the problem of storing sand and pallets of cement on-site and the risk of inconsistent mixing and quality control with hand-mixed screed. But ultimately, there were health issues for site workers with silica dust being the biggest problem when opening bags of cement."

"Roughly 24 months ago, we commenced working with a team of Australian and International engineers along with technology suppliers to develop a fully self-contained automatic screed mixing and pumping system," Les continued. "One of the many challenges was making the unit fit Australian ADR regulations. That's where Scania came to the party and became an integral partner in the development process. Their help actually made the process a whole lot easier."

"These new trailer pumps are fully self-contained, sealed systems for automatic mixing and pumping large volumes of 15 to 50 MPA screed up to 180 metres horizontally and 30 floors vertically," Les said.

"The tilers love our product because they can get the job done much faster, save time, cost and effort of sourcing raw materials along with the manual mixing and barrowing of screed," Les added. "Importantly, the safety officers love our machines and process because we have eliminated

high-risk manual handling and fully eliminated silica dust generation in the mixing of the screed."

Western Australia General Manager Kevin Andersen added that over the past three years, they've been at the forefront in developing engineered screeds. Today, their engineered screeds account for over 50 per cent of the screeds they supply.

"Architects, builders and tilers have embraced the significant benefits of these products, and we see this trend continuing to grow," Keven said. "Now, with our computer-controlled pump units, the mix of our products is engineered with precision and mixed with exacting consistency allowing us to provide a 10-year warranty on our products."

Eventually, by mid-2023, ScreedPro aims to have depots in all major capital cities. Currently, they have depots based in Perth, Melbourne and Sydney.

"We also service regional projects," Les explained. "That's the beauty of our system being truck-mounted. We can go virtually anywhere. In fact, last week, we sent one Scania P380 on a job 1,000km from Sydney on Sunday for a 13-m3 engineered screed job on Monday. That unit arrived back in Sydney ready for an apartment project by 7 am Tuesday morning. That's the beauty of the Scania P380's performance and reliability."

ScreedPro was looking for much more than the cheapest truck quote when selecting a truck supplier. They wanted a transport partner who would be deeply involved in the entire technology development process and fleet rollout. In this regard, Scania was the clear choice.

Les Stockdale comments that the Scania Team and the P380 prime movers play a significant role in the initial and ongoing success of their operation. "Throughout the development process, Scania has provided great assistance

Opposite Page: NSW General Manager Les Stockdale is happy with the productivity and safety gains the Scania and purpose-built trailer deliver.
Above Left: The manoeuvrability of the Scania and steerable trailer enables it to negotiate narrow urban laneways.
Above Right Top: The use of wide 385/65R22.5 super single tyres on BPW ECO Plus2 axle with pivoting hub and the Tridec suspension gives the trailer a greater steering angle.
Above Right Bottom: Additional steering via the wireless remote override system is used to get the trailer in and out of the tightest sites such as around this city building.

and not just delivered us a truck but a transport solution that integrated with and enhanced our pump trailer technology," Les said.

"They not only look after the service and maintenance of our Scania trucks, but they also carry out all the service and maintenance to our trailers' road running components. In addition, they work hand in hand with our specially trained team of engineers who provide the technical support for our mixing and pumping trailer units on the back of the trailers," he added.

"Scania suggested the P-series model to us because of its low-weight cabin with exceptional visibility," Les explained. "It had all the comfort and safety features we wanted to provide our drivers, like easy cabin access for urban work, a quiet working environment, and enough storage space for the odd long-haul trek. In addition, because of the high degree of technology and automation in our system, we had a number of technology requirements which Scania was proactive about incorporating into our build-up."

The NTG P380 certainly ticks all the boxes when it comes to urban driving, which often involves many stops and starts with repeated climbing in and out of the cabin. Because the cabin entrance is low, with convenient grab handles, this operation is straightforward and safer for the driver. Manoeuvring around tight construction sites requires exceptional concentration and visibility, and this is another area where the P380 shines. Because the driver sits high in the cabin, they have an outstanding vista forward through the broad curved windscreen and rearward via the wide mirror system. The motorised mirrors can be opportunely rotated to follow the trailer by use of the multifunction mirror switch conveniently located on the driver's side door armrest.

"There is no question the Scania P380 really is a premium workhorse," Les added. "When you consider the ease of cabin access, incredible storage options and sleeper area."

These ScreedPro P380 trucks are powered by Scania D13 380HP (283kW) engine coupled to a 14-speed overdrive transmission with Opticrusie shift.

Manoeuvring in and around tight city construction sites is right up the Scania P380's alley. Conversely, manoeuvring a standard-length tri-axle trailer in and around the same construction sites is a different story altogether. However, that's another area the ScreedPro team worked tirelessly on. To ensure their new trailers would match the manoeuvrability of the Scania P380, they had them custom-built to their exact specifications.

The addition of the Groeneveld auto grease canister fitted to the right-hand leg is probably the first sign an onlooker gets that there is some special running gear in this trailer that requires regular lubrication, and that's what prompts a further look underneath.

A quick glance at the skid plate on the trailer reveals the telltale signs of Jost's Tridec hydraulic steerable suspension. The system utilises a hydraulic linkage between the fifth wheel coupling plate and axle assemblies employing hydraulic cylinders. Besides, additional manoeuvrability can be achieved using the wireless remote manual override system to get the trailer in and out of the tightest sites.

BPW ECO Plus2 axle with a pivoting hub on either end of the axle is coupled to the Tridec steering suspension. The use of wide 385/65R22.5 super single tyres on the Tridec suspension gives the trailer a greater steering angle than if the traditional dual tyre were fitted. In addition, the trailer's smart braking system is a BPW-Wabco combination commonly found on many Australian-built trailers, which means parts commonality and maintenance is simplified.

This innovative Scania P380 and its state-of-the-art trailer are indeed pioneering a new approach to productivity, cost reduction, quality enhancement and workplace safety in not just the building industry but transport as well.

Insert: Scania's onboard scales display the axle weights on the dash.
Opposite: Screedpro's trailer set up pumping mixed screed onsite.
Below Left: The block on the skid plate that controls Jost's Tridec hydraulic steerable suspension.
Below Right: When the Scania turns the movement of the block in the mouth of the fifth wheel signals the trailer's hydraulic steering to activate.

TRUCK SPECIFICATIONS

Model:	Scania P380 6x4
Engine:	Scania DC13 380 13-Litre inline-6-Cylinder
Horsepower:	380 hp (283) kW @1900 RPM
Torque:	1400 lb/ft (1900Nm) @ 1000-1300 RPM
Gearbox:	Scania GRSO905R 14-speed Overdrive
Gearbox shift:	Opticruise
Retarder:	Scania R3500
Alternator:	Scania 24V 100amp
Compressor:	Knorr 720CR, twin cylinder, 800 L/min with air dryer
Propeller Shaft:	P604
Steering Box:	ZF8098 17-20:1
Front Axles:	Scania AM420S
Front Suspension:	2 x 32 Parabolic
Rear Axles:	Scania AD200SA axle housings
Rear Axle Ratio:	3.42:1 with diff locks to both axles
Rear Suspension:	Scania Air
Brakes:	Scania electronically controlled disc brakes
Tyres:	Bridgestone 295/80R22.5R
Safety:	EBS with integrated ABS and traction control
Wheelbase:	3150mm
Cab Tilt:	Electronic
Interior:	Vinyl & Textile Trim
Seats:	Medium driver's seat velour black
Battery Box:	2x12V, 180-amp Chassis mount LH side
Fuel Tank:	1 x 300L R/H side & 1 x 400L L/H side
Adblue tank:	1 x 80L R/H side

Trailer's Block

Scania: Trucking in Australia

More than just a Tonka Truck

Reduced fuel burn per kilometre and the efficient Scania Retarder were two key factors driving the recent purchase of a pair of Scania R 620 V8 rigid tippers by B&J Catalano in Bunbury, WA.

The company's new V8-powered 8x4 rigid tippers primarily haul silica sand from their quarry north of Bunbury into the town's port, passing through some residential areas, so the silent operation of the Scania Retarder provides a considerable advantage over other auxiliary braking systems.

"We needed to get through the suburbs as quietly as possible, so the Retarder really does help us out," says Mark Kingston, B&J Catalano's Fleet Manager.

"Fuel use in the first 70,000 km has been impressive too. We have achieved our target of 1.4 km per litre, an improvement over the 1.0 or 1.1km/l we used to achieve from our older trucks," he adds.

In addition to the fuel-saving and quiet operating Retarder, driver reports from behind the wheel speak of improved ergonomics and comfort, reducing fatigue.

"The reduction of fatigue is a benefit, but a bonus is the attendant improvement in driver alertness leading to improved safety on the job, plus reduced wear and tear on the equipment," Mark reveals.

B&J Catalano runs 80 trucks in its transport and bulk haulage business, and had never tried a Scania previously. However, a sub-contractor with a Scania talked up the performance of his vehicle. As a result, Mark reveals the company decided to invest in a couple of Scania trucks to chase fleet fuel savings.

"We wanted to see for ourselves what the Scania could do. We had seen how the sub-contractor's vehicle provided a superior performance on hills thanks to the Retarder. As soon as we put one of our drivers into the Scania, he loved it. He informed me that there are so many systems in the truck that it practically drives itself."

"We have the Adaptive Cruise Control fitted, which maintains safe following distances on the multi-lane road we travel on, and also Lane Departure Warning. The drivers understood that we had a fuel efficiency target with the Scanias, and one recently sent me a screenshot from the dash showing 1.4 km/l. This was indeed an encouraging result. With further driver training, we aim to achieve this target consistently."

"We have had a visit from the Scania Driver Trainers," Mark says. "Even though many of our drivers are very experienced, with decades on the road, they found the driver efficiency training very useful, particularly the fuel-saving tips. But, of course, this driver efficiency training translates to the other trucks we have in the fleet too."

"Now we have signed up for the Scania Driver Services Monitoring package, which gives us a weekly review of how the trucks have been performing and allows us to check the truck is running in economy mode, for example," Mark says.

> "there are so many systems in the truck that it practically drives itself."

The trucks run fully loaded from the quarry to the port precinct. It is only a short distance of around 50 km on mostly flat terrain, though up to seven round trips are made per shift. Most times, the trucks return empty, though they can shift loads from the port to the company's storage area if freight is available.

One of the new Scanias has been fitted with lightweight Graham Lusty trailers, allowing an even higher payload. The company is currently investigating the new Level 3 Concessional Mass Management limits in WA, aiming for a payload of up to 90 tonnes.

The second vehicle uses existing trailers, and a switch to lighter trailers could add up to 4-tonnes of potential payload, all of which helps bottom line profitability from full asset utilisation.

One of the vehicles has the trailers closely coupled, while the second uses longer A-frame drawbars to run at close to 36.5m.

"We have completed around 70,000 km so far in one of the trucks, and they will probably top out at around 120,000 km a year, which isn't huge mileage," Mark says. "We aim to keep the trucks for about ten years. We like to get the most effective economic utilisation out of the vehicle over its lifetime. We are committed to keeping our equipment in good condition, and we have an in-house workshop team that looks after all of our vehicles.

"The Scania team in Bunbury has looked after us very well. Roy Wallace has been very proactive, keeping us up-to-date and explaining the Scania maintenance intervals," Mark says.

"The two new Scanias are R620 8X4 rigid tippers pulling two road train trailers with a GVM of 130-tonnes," says Roy Wallace, New Truck Account Manager at Scania WA.

"We are delighted B&J Catalano has decided to give the Scania trucks a go in their mixed fleet of European and American trucks. Furthermore, we are pleased that the R 620s are living up to their reputation of delivering impressive fuel consumption and high levels of driver comfort."

Scania has a global reputation for efficiency and reliability. Its experience building trucks for mining and resources companies means that there will be a Scania to suit whatever the size of the job. An 8x4 rigid, pulling two 6-axle trailers, might amaze European road users. The Scania design teams locally and globally understand what operators like B&J Catalano need to get the job done.

Scania: Trucking in Australia

Hauling 100 tonnes with a 100 per cent driver score, banker-turned-trucker Ken Beggs looks after the cents with his fully-maintained R 730. With a degree in Agricultural Science and Accounting, Ken Beggs may be Australia's most educated truckie.

At 18, he started driving trucks and was also involved in farming, but his life took a major turn at 21 when an accident left him with broken bones in his neck and in a quadriplegic state for some time.

Trucking and farming were no longer options. So while in his mid 30's and with a young family to provide for, Ken took himself to university and, over five years, earned his degrees and moved into banking.

"I worked with a number of the major banks, which meant moving around a bit and reasonably quickly moved from farm business banking into corporate and institutional banking in the agribusiness sector," Ken said.

"I don't know if I was cut out to be a banker, but I had a lot of empathy with the Agri sector, and there is no doubt my qualifications and experience helped me to talk with farmers and institutional rural businesses. As a result, I progressed to a position of State Manager of a division of one of the major banks."

Despite the ongoing success, Ken felt pressured to make another career change at age 55 when the bank industry thought he had come to the end of his useful life. So he

reluctantly left banking and retired for about 15 minutes before getting bored.

At this time, his son was driving trucks and offered to take him for a ride. Initially, he resisted as he loved trucks too much but eventually went for a ride in an American truck. Unfortunately, it was so rough it badly aggravated his neck injury. Sometime later, his son took him for a ride in a European truck which proved much smoother and more comfortable.

"I was hooked again," Ken said, following that second ride. "So I bought a European truck about ten years ago and did steel work for Linfox and some linehaul work for Border Express to get a handle on operating costs and things. Then I went out on my own doing tipper work in my other love, the agricultural sector."

Once his last truck reached 1.2 million kilometres, it was time for a new one. So he purchased a new Scania R 730 to treat himself.

"I've always had small trucks doing big jobs," Ken said, "and as this is my last truck, I figured I'm going to finish in a big way in the biggest truck Australia has to offer and the biggest set of trailers in the south-eastern part of Australia. I think I'm still the only one with a permit to operate A-B triples in Victoria," Ken said (at the time of writing).

The Scania R 730 features a unique colour scheme. Ken had only previously owned white trucks. "My sons told me white looks a bit boring," Ken said, "but I wasn't going to cover it in lights, chrome or pinstripes as I reckon that's a bit old-fashioned."

"I have to thank Paul Riddell at Scania Adelaide," said Ken. "He put me in touch with a painter, Paul from Mikutta's in Adelaide, who did a brilliant job painting the truck and, in turn, engaged a guy who specialises in airbrushing Harley Davidsons. At first, the airbrushing guy wasn't interested, but when I showed him my concept, he agreed, providing I gave him some artistic licence."

The distinctive paint job isn't the only unique feature of Ken's Scania R 730. There's the sizable bullbar, for one thing. Driving well into the night, Ken said that kangaroos in western NSW have been seen in plague proportions for years, and collecting one each trip is not uncommon.

'Roos destroyed the first bull bar on his last truck in no time, and despite replacing it with a heavier one, the same fate befell it.

The eye-catching artwork on the R 730 cab certainly makes this a stand-out truck if the three trailers didn't already make enough of a statement.

> "My sons told me white looks a bit boring"

Scania: Trucking in Australia

Top: To achieve additional payload Ken has his Scania enrolled in the NHRV Intelligent Access Program (IAP). This device monitors Ken's axle weights and the roads he travels to ensure he is complying with is permit conditions.

Above: The central tyre inflation monitor displays the actual tyre pressure and lets Ken adjust the tyre pressure simply by selecting the appropriate button for the load.

So with the R730, Ken enlisted help from Chris Barron in Adelaide, who came up with a different design that is proving more effective. The Scania also features a forward-facing radar system used for the adaptive cruise control, but after it was destroyed by 'roos and repaired twice, Ken has covered it up with a heavy plate.

Operating between the Murray region of Victoria and South Australia and southwest Queensland, Ken primarily carts stock feed to feedlots and occasionally feedmills. With an all-up weight of just over 100 tonnes and with up to 65 tonnes of payload, Ken and his R 730 clock up around 200,000 km each year.

Ken commissioned Graham Lusty Trailers of Queensland to build his large-capacity custom tipping trailers and dolly and said they were terrific to work with and have done an excellent job. Each of the four triaxle groups is fitted with Knorr Bremse EBS/ABS braking along with a stability roll-over system, which complements the Scania's advanced braking system.

Ken uses Scania's fleet monitoring service, with its operational rating system, which is 'bloody addictive' according to him, as he constantly tries to beat his previous score. However, the program needs to be modified to suit the conditions the R 730 operates in.

"I usually score between 98 and 99 over the period of a week, but one week I achieved the perfect '100' and was very proud of that," he said.

Being pragmatic about operating his business, Ken also has the Scania Premium Maintenance Program and appreciates that repairs, maintenance and servicing costs move from being an unpredictable and unknown variable cost to a known fixed cost.

"If you happen to encounter a breakdown on the road, Scania, come out and fix it wherever you are. One call to Scania takes so much worry out of the business, and if you have a problem, you move it to somebody else as it's already been paid for in your monthly fee," Ken said.

With a percentage of his return trips, empty Ken has installed a tyre inflation system on the drive wheels and trailers, so the tyre pressures are inflated or deflated to run at their optimum pressure, thereby extending their life. Just another way Ken reduces his running costs.

Even though (at the time of writing) it was early days for Ken and his Scania R 730, we asked him how it stacks up so far.

"The power is fantastic, and it easily pulls the 100-tonnes along like my old 540 pulled a B-double," Ken says. "It's very comfortable like all European trucks. It's a straightforward truck to drive and very simple to operate.

"I have added a microwave oven in the sleeper section, and the second bunk is used for storage because when you live in a truck, you need that extra storage space. Plus, I have an in-bunk air conditioner to make sleeping on hot nights a bit easier. It is the first one I've had, and it's a bit of luxury that I enjoy.

" Another couple of reasons for choosing the R 730 are that it's Euro 6 compliant while others were only Euro 5, and I reckon that will help its resale value. Another reason was the retarder that I think is a very clever idea and works brilliantly on the roads I use," he said.

Scania: Trucking in Australia

R730
Floats on

A big job demands a big truck. And for Matt Winterfield, in the past, that job has always been done by a big used truck. But not anymore. Now a brand new Scania R 730 V8 undertakes the task of hauling farming, earthmoving and logging heavy machinery around Mount Gambier, the far eastern corner of South Australia and western Victoria. So what has bought this change for a rural businessman with more than 25 years of experience under his belt?

"We're a family-owned heavy haulage company," Matt says. "We're contracted to move other people's gear. About 85 per cent of the work is forestry-related, with the rest farming and earthmoving.

"I've been in the industry 25-30 years, and trucks all my life. I'm a mechanic by trade, and I grew up around trucks. My dad was a truck driver. In fact, my whole family work in the forestry industry.

"We run two prime movers and two low loaders. We have this new Scania now, and once my other truck gets sold, I'm getting one, too.

"We have never bought brand new trucks as we have always run second-hand prime movers. But the repair and maintenance costs are very high on second-hand equipment. So I figured the only way to fix the repair and maintenance issue is to go new, and Scania fitted the bill," Matt adds.

"I have never liked Euro trucks, I've always been American-based, but things have come a long way from when I last had anything to do with European lorries. The Americans have dropped the ball. They're not even close. So in the big picture, Scania is way ahead on all counts.

"We looked at all the Europeans, and we felt the Scania the best on the market, for our application, you can tell by the way they are finished.

"Our business strategy is to stay in front of our maintenance, and with second-hand equipment, it has proved impossible. But now, with a new Scania and the Maintenance & Repair contract, we know exactly what expense we're up for, and not waiting for another big bill at the end of the month," he says.

"I have been paying off a second-hand American truck and also paying for repairs as they have come up. Recently the repair costs have been getting out of hand. So, working with Paul Riddell from Scania in Adelaide, we structured a package that includes maintenance and repairs on the R 730."
"This gives me full transparency of my truck costs over the term. In addition, it allows me to plan my cash flow and deal out any unpleasant surprises at the end of the month. And

Driver's View

Peter 'Darkie' O'Dea is a fair dinkum salt of the earth Australian icon. His straightforward call-it-like he sees it attitude is refreshingly direct. Never short of a rapier-like one-liner, he'll bring a wide grin to any group. Peter's past life included stints in the national rodeo circus, assisted by his imposing tall timber stance and whip-crack reactions. Best not to creep up on him then.

If ever there was to be an advocate for traditional old-style trucking, you'd imagine Peter as the figurehead, and so it was. But no longer. With only a few thousand km under the wheels of his new R 730, 'Darkie' is converted.

"There's not much to not like," he says in a legendary, laconic way. "It is a pleasure to get into this truck.

"Everything is easy. Excellent vision is the first thing you notice

from the driver's seat. They haven't just thrown mirrors on the side for the sake of having them there. Comfort is a big thing. The bed is good, and I have had a few nights in it. I was in Melbourne overnight a few weeks ago, and it snowed. It's a well-insulated cab because, in the morning, it was just as warm as it was when I turned in, that's unusual.

But I guess this truck comes from a country that's used to a bit of snow. The sleeping area lights can be switched off when you're in bed. That's another bonus.

"It's quiet on the road. So I have taken to listening to the radio again. I haven't listened to the radio for years for the simple reason that I couldn't hear it in the last truck.

"At the end of the day, I feel a lot better. Although I was crook in the back for the first week, only because now I was sitting straight behind the wheel, whereas in the past, the steering wheel was offset by two inches, so I was twisted all day. Now I am good as gold all day.

"A typical day is long. There's a lot of loading and unloading and a lot of driving. We'll do 5-or-6 deliveries on a busy day, and we load 80 per cent of the gear ourselves. So the trick to loading this machinery is the slower you are, the better you are.

"I like getting in and out of the Scania; you can manage it without spilling your coffee.

"Initially, we were worried about the ride height for the bush work, but through the wet season, it has been no trouble. "I'm a fan of the Scania Retarder. It's a whole new world. I've only ever had a Jake brake before, and they're only good for scaring old folks and wild animals. This retarder is much better. I'm watching the scores on the Driver Support readout on the dash. I got up to 98 per cent on braking, pretty happy with that.

"I went into Adelaide loaded the other day, set the speed at 50, held it there. In the past, you'd slow it to 20 kph down Mount Lofty, then let it run up, and then slow it again. Whereas the Scania just sat on 50 kph, and away we went.

"These Drake trailers Matt has bought with their rear steering axles let you go around corners a lot tighter because you're not dragging them. They've saved him more than he paid to put on them in the first year compared with his old float.

"With a load like this, John Deere, it doesn't actually feel like you have anything behind you. It's only about 26-tonne. The old girl (previous truck) would have known it was there, but this thing just goes. It doesn't seem to matter what you have on it.

"It does have to grunt sometimes, though. I was going into the bush the other day, and we had a chipper on, right up on my weights, probably 80-tonne, and I could feel the trailer in the spongy ground, but I never needed to alter the accelerator; it just started to grunt, and away it went. It fair blew me away. And it's only doing 1500 revs at 100 km/h."

Scania: Trucking in Australia

then there's the performance bonus of the R 730 V8."

"We move a lot of large equipment, and with oversize, over-mass machines in the past, you couldn't always keep up to the speed limit, dropping back in the hills. So we needed extra power, and we got that with the R 730 V8.

"I've never had a truck with too much power until now," he says with his trademark grin. "I have been very impressed with the Scania's performance," Matt adds.

"Peter O'Dea has been working for me for a long time, and he is the regular driver of the Scania. We both loaded at the exact location a few days ago, and I headed off well before him. I couldn't believe it when he caught me up, and of course, he chirped over the radio that I must have a trailer brake locked on. Well, I hadn't. That Scania he was driving was powering up the hills, and I couldn't get away from him.

"Another day, we headed towards Ballarat out of Melbourne and came past a B-double up the hills. The driver of the B-double couldn't believe we had breezed past him up the hill. We were astonished because he said he was running empty, although we were pulling a loaded trailer. We didn't

Left: Hauling heavy and oversized loads is Winterfield's speciality. As a result, the company is well known throughout the Mount Gambier region.

Right: Peter 'Darkie' O'Dea cites the Scania R730 as true driver's truck.

get any more chirps out of that guy after that. That's the difference the Scania makes," Matt says. "We're getting excellent trip times because we're not slowing on the hills.

"One of my core business goals is to find the gear that helps me stay in front of the market," he adds. "The 50-tonne Drake trailer is a good example. I had this one specified with self-steering rear axles. The cost saving in tyres has already paid for the additional cost over a standard trailer. Where tyres on the rear were lasting only 45,000 km on fixed axles, I have had 175,000 km out of these. Saves money and downtime having them replaced."

The new Scania is eye-catching and very smartly turned out. In addition to the stripe kit, there are chrome highlights and V8 badging, as well as chromed Chris Barron mudguards, and a catwalk set between the long-range tanks that hold 1100-litres of fuel and a 75-litre AdBlue tank.

"Matt has made a big statement by coming to Scania," says Paul Riddell, New Truck Account Manager at Scania Wingfield.

"He's come to us after identifying what he wants from his truck, studying the market, and making a business decision. With his Maintenance and Repair programme, Matt's got peace of mind and knows what his costs are, and best of all, for his business, his driver loves the experience.

"I'm looking forward to delivering Matt another R 730 V8, and this one he is going to drive himself," Paul says.

Scania: Trucking in Australia

Drake Steering Widener Low-Loader

D rake's Steering Widener low-loader range of trailers offers all the benefits of their deck widener range with the added advantage of enhanced stability, improved manoeuvrability and reduced tyre wear. One of the shortcomings with a full deck widener low-loader is the excessive scrubbing of the trailer tyres on turns, primarily due to the far wider track of the axles when the unit is in the fully extended position. However, on the plus side, the wider track of the axles allows for increased trailer stability when carrying wide-heavy equipment.

However, Drake's 4x4 Steering Widener low loader is most suited to transporting machines like the Terex Pegson XR400 mobile crusher because the deck quickly widens to suit the track width of the machine. Furthermore, the trailing two-axle groups remain in the standard position, similar to the deck widener model. In contrast, the leading two axle groups extend outwards with the deck to provide increased stability when carrying the larger machines.

Self-tracking BPW axles make manoeuvring around tight bends and twisting roads much easier on the trailer and improve tyre wear compared to fixed axle units. Additionally, there is minimal impact on the road surface.

The Steering Widener low loader has one group of axles that extend outwards with the deck width for optimum stability. And that the trailing axles run at a narrower track means that when the low-loader is required to move to the left to pass oncoming traffic, the trailing axle group remain on the hard bitumen surface, which adds to the vehicle's stability.

These Drake Steering Widener low-loaders boast an extensive list of standard features, including stainless steel hydraulic tubing, which has proven trouble-free for decades. The complete trailer is grit blasted and painted in 2-pack paint to the customer's requirements. The lighting is all LED, while the braking is electronic EBS with ABS and roll stability. The sliding skid plate means that achieving optimum axle weights is easy for the operator, regardless of the load dimensions or machine on the low-loader or whether a dolly is combined.

A standard feature often used in extreme heavy going is the push point location at the rear of the low-loader when a pusher unit is required to connect to the combination.

The ramps are hydraulically controlled and use the same onboard 6.5hp hydraulic power pack to operate the deck

widening system and raise or lower the gooseneck. There are two spare wheel carriers located on the gooseneck, an alloy water tank and a dunnage tray. There are dual lockable toolboxes down either side of the trailer.

Specification-wise, the 4 x 4 Drake Steering Widener low-loader has a 50-tonne capacity, and the deck extends from its standard travelling width of 2.5-meters to 3.5-meters. The trailer has a 13-meter deck length with 3.05-meter-long ramps.

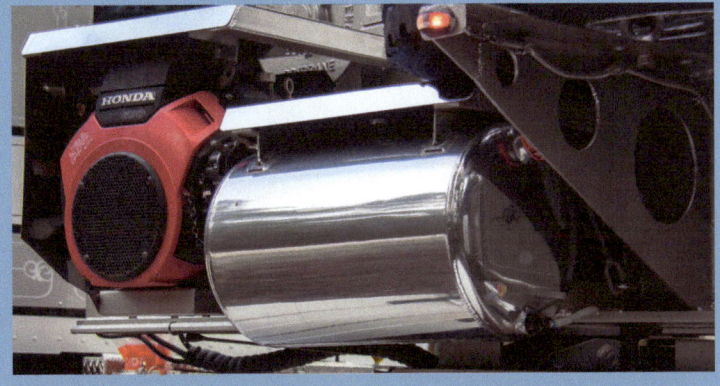

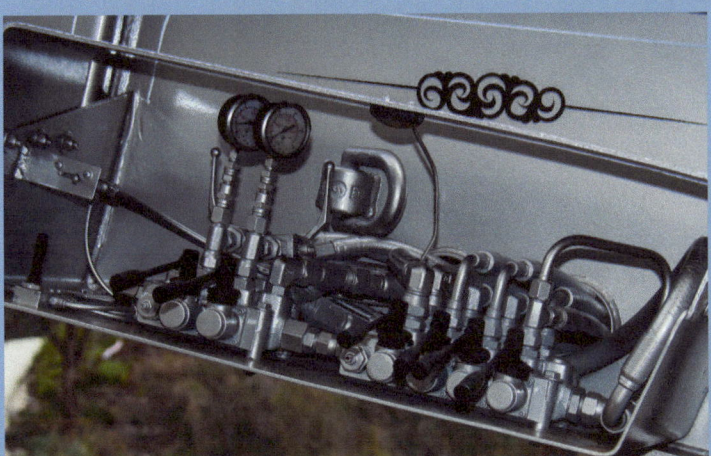

Top Left: Gooseneck mounted hydraulic winch.

Bottom Left: Gooseneck mounted hydraulic controls.

Top Right: Honda power pack engine with Alloy water tank.

Middle Right: Chain boxes integrated into deck.

Bottom Right: Turn-buckle storage in the gooseneck.

Left: The Drake trailer has steerable rear axles, which have helped extend tyre life considerably.

LOW LOGGER & TRACTION

Elphinstone Low Logger, Central Tyre Inflation and Scania's big hub reduction rear axles boost productivity for South Australian logging contractor Hans Scheidl.

A cold, crisp morning in a pine forest is one of the most natural places in the world to find a V8-powered Scania truck and a set of logging trailers. Scania's logging industry spurs were hard-won decades ago in Scandinavian forests ranging from the edge of the Artic to the base of the Baltic peninsular.

So the strengths of Scania's all-steel-safety engineered cab's plentiful power and torque, boosted by excellent traction through loamy, boggy, crudely-cut roads and snow-covered tracks, shine through just as brightly in the heart of South Australia's carefully managed woodlands as they do, back where the Scanias were designed.

Just outside Mount Gambier, there is a broad mix of nature and juvenile pine forest plantations, interspersed with cleared acreages replanted with new saplings. It's a veritable production line of forest worked over decades-long lifecycles.

H & L Scheidl is a well-known livestock and logging contractor that has been based in Mount Gambier for 22 years, though owners Hans and Lill have been involved in the industry much longer.

"I started working at 15 with my uncle in the logging industry," Hans says, seated comfortably at the kitchen table in the company office on the town's outskirts.

"The choice was fishing or logging, and I'm not keen on holding a line, so logging became my only option. My first truck was a Benz, but that was a long time ago."
Since establishing this business, Hans has revolved through several American and European truck brands but has now found Scania the solution to his logging trailer toting needs.

"Since we have had the Scanias, they have just worked. So I haven't been getting calls from drivers stuck with a broken down truck, and I haven't been suffering trucks off the roads for weeks waiting for parts, or bits just falling off during day-to-day operations," he says in his no-nonsense way.

The Scanias have eliminated my downtime," Hans adds. "This is vital because this business is all about volume."

"The engines and gearboxes are good, and the servicing has been great. We have one 620HP truck that has done 120,000 km and another with 60,000 km. I needed trucks that work in the bush, and these work well there. They have given me no grief at all," Hans says.

"Alfons Reitsma of Scania Adelaide specked the trucks well. He knew what he was doing, as he understands logging," Hans reveals.

"The Scanias have provided excellent traction in the muddy and slippery forest roads, thanks to their hub-reduction axles on 4-point air," he says. "We also went for 14-speed manual synchromesh gearboxes because they are easy to drive and the drivers like them.

"We specified the new Scania 4100 Nm retarder for the R620s, that gives us plenty of breaking performance. Our trucks had the first of the big Retarders in Australia," Hans says with some pride."

"I have driven a few loads with this Retarder activated, and it is awesome. Unlike a Jake Brake, you can still change gear when the Retarder is working," Hans informs.

Operating a fleet of American and some European trucks, the reaction from the Scheidl driver group was almost universally positive when the Scania trucks arrived.

"One of my drivers, Jim Smith, says he feels better getting out of the Scania after a shift than when he got in," Hans says.

"At present, Hans has three Scania R620s working in the forests nearby. They're loading over a long working day and delivering logs either to the local mill in Mt Gambier or in Portland or Colac, each of which are several hundred km away.

"The Scanias are the only trucks I am double shifting at present," Hans says. "They are good for this."

A typical load is 44.5 tonnes of logs for a 68-tonne GCM. The pine logs are carried on Elphinstone trailers with an advanced strapping system, onboard scales and EBS. The trailer is tough enough to handle the loads, and the forest floor tracks and the white metal roads are stable enough to give drivers confidence when operating close to posted speed limits.

"The bottom line for us is that the Scanias deliver very high productivity," Hans says.

CTI Tyre Inflation system

The Scheidl Scania R620s are fitted with an advanced New Zealand sourced tyre inflation system (Traction Air) with integrated GPS that allows the driver to concentrate on his driving rather than worrying about adjusting his tyre pressures as he moves in and out of the forests.

After testing in Schiedl's operating conditions, the company has developed a specific hub-end package for Scanias fitted with hub reduction systems that manage heat effectively, enhancing the working life of the CTI wheel end rotators, which in turn, increases productivity for the customer.

The tyre pressure management system works with limited input from the driver. Re-inflation gets triggered by the GPS receiver, which measures the vehicle's ground speed independent of the speedometer. This ensures safety by first alerting the driver about his speed relative to the pressure setting. Should the driver not increase the pressure to the next stage, the system automatically increases the tyre pressure to the next step.

Traction Air CTI is fully programable, and settings can be tailored to a specific application to optimise protection against overheating, excess wear and excess fuel use.

When running at low pressure over slippery terrain, the rubber footprint is significantly increased, which is good for added traction should you need it over cross locks and traction control.

...continued Page-89

Driver's View

Dave Jones has been driving logging trucks in the forests outside Mount Gambier for around three years. He averages about 300 km daily, making multiple runs from the forest log-loading areas to the local mill.

"The open-air attracted me. There's a lot less traffic here. I was on fuel before this, which was very hectic. The stress level is gone, as seen in our work environment. "It's quiet and peaceful here.

My first Scania experience was about six years ago when I was still doing fuel deliveries. We had one of the first trucks with the retarder system, which was great.

"What I like most about the Scania is that when you get to my age, and you have been driving for a long time, you tend to think about comfort.

"After a 14-hour day in the Scania, you get out and feel great. Your back is not all twisted up because the truck is just so comfortable. Plus, the heated seats in this environment are great," he says, gesturing to the torrential rain sluicing through the trees on a day when the mercury can't even hope to reach double figures.

We're hauling 44 tonnes of logs, and the ride is very smooth.

"I like the low revving high torque performance of the 620HP. It reminds me of an old Mack V8. The Scania motor likes working in the 1000-1400 rpm range; that's the sweetspot. Anything over that, and you're wasting fuel and time," he says.

"I have found the Scania retarder to be absolutely brilliant. I pretty much only touch the service brakes right at the end of the braking cycle. Depending on circumstances, I'm using the Retarder for about 85 per cent of the braking in a day, and it really does make life easier, especially on the fatigue side.

"Another Scania benefit is the visibility. Compared to a bonneted truck, the Scania has a really widescreen and none of those air cleaners or stacks in your vision, and it does make a big difference, especially in this environment and at night as well. The truck also has a very tight turning circle, another benefit in the forest," Dave adds.

"At the end of the day, it's just how you feel when you get out. And it's great."

Driver's View

Above Left: Jim Smith, straps up the load and gets some exercise at the same time.

Above: Jim Smith finds the Scania very comfortable to drive.

Below: This CTI Tyre Inflation solution was explicitly devised for H & L Scheidl's business and provides an advanced and sophisticated monitoring system designed to extend tyre life in arduous working conditions

Jim Smith is relatively new to the Scania driving experience, with only a few months behind the wheel when we dropped by. Despite his long driving experience, this is his first stint in a Scania. But it has not taken him long to appreciate the benefits.

"I found the Scania to be very comfortable. It tracks beautifully as well," he adds.

Jim's main run is a return trip to Colac most nights, which is a 750 km round trip. As a warm-up, he often does a few short runs from the forest to the Mount Gambier mill, dropping 44 tonnes of logs before heading off towards the Victorian town to the east.

"Like my shift partner, Dave, I am a fan of the Retarder. I use it all the time," he adds. "The Scania is sure-footed in the forest and gives us great traction."

Scania: Trucking in Australia

Above: The 620 HP V8 power is ideally suited to logging applications.

Below: Hans has opted for a traditional vertical exhaust stack on his log trucks.

The CTI system recognises when the need for low-pressure driving has ended and reinflates the tyres for normal road running. The system can also detect a leak in a tyre and alert the driver while using the auxiliary compressor to continue feeding air to the leaking tyre.

Sensors constantly monitor the pressure in tyres, adjusting hot and cold tyres to optimum settings to ensure longer tyre life.

Gavin Hailey, National Sales Manager of Tidd Rodd Todd, the company supplying the Traction Air CTI system for Scanias, says it is an essential element of the vehicle's off-highway performance.

"We believe this system can benefit more than logging contractors: bulk tippers, livestock carters and pretty much any operator who is spending time off-highway can use it. It is relatively maintenance-free, requiring only periodic inspections," Gavin says.

Scania Adelaide

Scania's Alfons Reitsma adds that Hans and Lill set very firm operating parameters when shopping for new trucks.

"They told us they wanted high productivity in terms of trip times and the ability to take the loads they are pulling from the forests, but critically tare weight, reliability, durability, safety and ground-clearance were important vital factors. The way the logging industry is structured here in Australia, you must keep your trucks on the road as long as possible, hauling as much as possible. Using the Scania engineered-in excellence program to meet the needs of the logging industry, we were confident our trucks could carry Han's load.

"We have a unique logging specification that includes a strong CA6x4MHA chassis. Up front is a straight 9-tonne front axle as well as essential safety features such as roll stability, ESP, EBS and built-in load scales, all of which help the drivers to do their jobs better and in greater safety. In addition, there is a high front bumper-bullbar, and the hub reduction over axle ratio of 3.67:1 allows outstanding take-off traction.

"We added Goodyear 385/65 R22.5 Super-singles as well to increase stability on the rough roads," Alfons says.

"Scania's logging spec truck is the ideal solution for forestry hauliers because of our Scandinavian logging expertise, plus our complete in-house engineering, our safety and of course V8 power, mean there is nothing better to do the bob. Hans Scheidl's experience with the V8s proves that," Alfons adds.

Left: Elphinstone Easyweigh remote handheld onboard vehicle weighing systems enables operators to monitor their axle weights during the loading procedure.

Below: Elphinstone air load binder-winch is an air operated auto tensioner. It has a lashing capacity of 5000 kg. Tested to AS/NZS-4380:2001 Motor Vehicles – Cargo Restraint Systems. The Elphinstone Auto-Tensioner winch will take-up tension on the strap and maintain constant pressure on the strap. If the load moves or compacts, the winch will automatically rachet around to maintain constant tension. Furthermore, if there is any problem with the air supply or controls, the winch automatically locks as if it is a manual winch. In addition, the winch can be used as a manual winch.

Southern Regional Transport (SRT) is a well-known grain carting company based in the southwest region of Western Australia. SRT shareholder Alan Moyle has 35 years of driving experience under his belt, and he acquired a brand new truck and three trailers, all conceived with one aim in mind, to become more efficient and productive. Moving up from his previous 90-tonnes gross combination mass truck pulling two-grain trailers, he opted for a third trailer and a more powerful truck to pull the now 130-tonne GCM 60-wheeler road train.

The selection of a twin-steer prime mover enables him to spread the front axle weight more evenly and cope with the high overall combination weight. It also gives him a more stable platform for driving on some of the less-than-smooth roads found in the Albany region.

While Alan's shiny new white R 730 V8 does without a traditional Aussie bullbar, it includes a stainless steel front bumper unit to ward off wayward animals potentially encountered on the state's roads.

During the planning stage, Alan and the engineers carefully calculated the combination's dimensions and accurately built the trailers to ensure the combination remained within the legislated maximum length limits; going without a bullbar meant additional capacity in the trailers on every load every day.

"With a bullbar, I would have been right on the 36-metre limit, but the steel bumper means I have 500 mm to play with and less weight over the front axle," Alan says.

Alan also went top shelf with his trailer specification, adding disc brakes and Alcoa rims to the specially constructed Evertrans end-tipper trailers.

With three trailers, Alan now carts 84 tonnes per load (121 tonnes gross) instead of 62 tonnes (90-tonnes gross), a significant increase in payload, earning more per trip, offset, of course, against the additional expense of the third trailer.

"Every extra kilo makes a difference when you are paid by weight," Alan says.

"In a typical 60-hour working week, we will be travelling around 4500 km," he says.

SRT runs 25 road trains and, along with another transport company, the two businesses operate 40 vehicles and jointly cart around 5000 tonnes of grain per day for Co-operative Bulk Handling, one of WA's largest grain companies. SRT collect grain from farms, deliver to silos during harvest time, and collect from silos and deliver to the port in Albany, Australia's most southerly grain export terminal, during the rest of the year.

CBH is the biggest cooperative in the Australian grain industry. It stores, handles and transports more than 85 per cent of WA's annual grain harvest and exports it to more than 20 global markets and domestic customers. In 2021, WA's growers delivered the fourth largest crop in history, with 13.52 million tonnes received by CBH. Hard-working rigs for rough roads

"Typically, we will cover around 700 km per day for five or six days each week," Alan says. "We'll work six days a week for the next six months. We're affected by the global market demand for grain. If the price is up, we need to shift it out of the silos and onto ships to get it sold as quickly as possible. Our location in the southern hemisphere means we must get our grain to market before the USA harvest comes in."

After travelling 18,000 km in the new Scania R 730 V8 in the first two months, Alan is achieving 1.55 km per litre, a meaningful improvement on the older trucks his colleagues are using for similar runs. However, Scania's AdBlue consumption appears initially to be about the same.

By Christmas, Alan expects to reach 150,000 km in the R 730, giving him far more data to analyse for a better understanding of his total running costs.

"I aim to keep this truck for about five years and will probably cover 700,000 km in that time," he concludes.

Steady as she goes
In the meantime, the experienced driver is enjoying the comfort and quietness of the Scania cab. Unusually, his partner Ellie Evans often accompanies Alan on his runs. Even more unusual is the fact that she often drives Alan's road train on return journeys.

"I haven't let anyone other than Ellie drive the truck yet," Alan says. Ellie is delighted to be driving the new Scania and says she has been driving trucks as long as she has known Alan for over 20 years.

"The Scania is a unique experience. I love the fact I believe I am the only woman carting grain in the southwest (of WA). "The stability of the truck on the road is fantastic for me. I feel very secure in this vehicle. I love driving it," she says. "When I take the bends, it is very stable."

"The best features so far are the quietness and the ride comfort," Alan says. "My last truck was European, so it was also quiet and comfortable. That was my first European truck, but that company couldn't supply a more powerful unit, so I looked around and turned to Scania.

"I chose the Scania above the rest for its fuel economy and power. Fuel efficiency and the economy is number one for me with the fuel cost now," he says. "The overall package is good, really," Alan says of the new R 730. "I use the retarder often, and the Opticruise is always in 'Auto'. Up the hills, however, we slip it into 'Power' mode, then on the return journey, we're in 'economy'," he says.

The journeys are pretty hilly, so power is in demand to pull such a substantial payload along at a reasonable speed.

"It is a very testing driving environment," Alan says. "It is quite hilly, and when you have trucks ahead of you and

Top: Alan and Ellie make a unique team.
2nd From Top: Ellie likes the comfort and ease of driving the R730
3rd From Top: Alan enjoys the power and economy of the R730
Above: That stainless steel bumper looks good and provides 500mm tolerance to the combination length.

Scania: Trucking in Australia

Shifting Western Australia's grain harvest is no mean task. The trucks are on the road carting grain from farms to silos and from silos to ports. Alan added an extra trailer when switching to Australia's most powerful truck because when you are paid by the kilo, the more you carry, the more you earn, so his productivity is increased significantly. At the silo, grain is checked for quality and pests as it comes off the truck.

behind you, you can't be holding them up. So you have to keep up." Unfortunately, according to Alan, the southwest of WA does not offer smooth, wide or well-maintained roads.

"They have been neglected a bit over the past 40 years," Alan says. "They are patched up and need some work. But instead, the authorities appear focused on enforcement, with weights and speed being the focus, rather than the building of safer roads.

"I am talking to Scania about fitting wider 'super singles' to the truck's steer axles to help keep it on the tar. We drive down very narrow roads with minimal bitumen surface past the white line, and once you drop off the edge with three trailers on, it is tough to get back. You don't want three loaded trailers steering you on the dirt above 80 km/h," he says.

According to Scania Kewdale, New Truck Account Manager Martin Grasett, Alan focused on his economic and highly productive truck requirements.

"Alan came to us wanting to be able to pull bigger payloads to get a higher level of productivity from his working week.

"With the power and torque of the Scania flagship R 730 V8, we can deliver more productivity and maintain impressive fuel consumption. We hope that Alan's success with the R 730 will lead to more sales of vehicles of this specification in the Albany region in the grain hauling industry," Martin says.

Scania: Trucking in Australia

The Evolution of Scania Opticruise G33-CM

Scania is certainly one manufacturer at the forefront in this field when it comes to developing a transmission that swaps cogs autonomously. In fact, Scania pioneered AMT (automated manual transmission) shift technology with their first incarnation of the Opticruise, released in 1995, which pre-dated ZF's AS-Tronic by a few years and Volvo's I-Shift by more than six years. However, while both Volvo and ZF abandoned the clutch pedal right from the beginning, Scania, on the other hand, was unwilling to do this initially. As a result, the two-pedal Opticruise eventually arrived on the market in 2009. Since then, its control strategies have constantly been evolving, with Scania regularly adding new functions and refinements.

The original Opticruise transmission differed significantly from rival automated boxes such as AS-Tronic, I-Shift and Mercedes' PowerShift gearboxes because of its traditional manual gearbox design links. The original Opticruise was truly an automated manual transmission (AMT). Hence it retained the synchroniser cones for the three main gears. On the other hand, the rival gearboxes are non-synchro designs and rely on electronic speed matching of the gears for shifts. Furthermore, the Opticruise's automatic clutch uses electro-hydraulic actuation, whereas the others are electro-pneumatic. Scania maintains both these characteristics aid shift quality and smoothness in off-road conditions.

Consequently, this makes the Opticruise an appealing option for vocational applications like logging, tippers, etc. Furthermore, Scania argues that the synchronisers make it easier and inflict less stress on the gearbox when performing a down-shift for engine braking on a steep downhill gradient.

The manoeuvring mode, introduced with two-pedal Opticruise in 2009, heralded improved yard manoeuvrability. This feature modifies the action of clutch engagement for more precise control when making small, low-speed movements. Before this introduction, manoeuvring was a weak point with early automated systems, not only in Opticruise but across the board. In actual fact, our recent road tests indeed confirm that this is no longer the case with Opticruise.

While some vocational operators are reluctant to specify an AMT transmission for fear that wheelspin in slippery off-road conditions often fools automated gearboxes into making unwanted upshifts, this is not the case with Opticruise because it senses speed from the front wheels.

Economy or power?
In the spring of 2013, Scania introduced two significant additions to Opticruise. Firstly, Scania Active Prediction (SAP), the GPS-enabled cruise control function, was integrated into Opticruise rather than being offered separately. Second, the addition of a new economy mode for Opticruise, joining the three other modes already available – standard, power and off-road.

Now Scania buyers have the flexibility to specify three of the four modes when ordering a new truck. The driver merely toggles between each mode using a switch on the steering

column's right-hand stalk to set the desired mode to suit the prevailing conditions.
Scania described the new mode as "tuned for maximum fuel-saving for long-distance haulage" when introducing economy mode".

There are subtle nuances between economy mode and standard mode in many respects. For example, the kick-down function is automatically disabled, and a lower speed limiter setting is activated when switching into economy mode. Hill-climbing shifting strategy also changes. Conversely, in standard mode and cruise control, the truck may accelerate before a hill climb if it calculates that this would reduce the number of downshifts required on the grade. While operating in economy mode and cruise control, there is never a speed increase before a hill because it is marginally more economical to avoid this, albeit at the expense of a few minutes.

In economy and standard modes, cruise control reduces the throttle input before a downhill descent to encourage the vehicle to start coasting, and it loses speed before the hill. The speed loss is up to 6 per cent below the cruise control's set speed in standard mode but as much as 12 per cent below in economy mode – a bone of contention among many drivers who feel progress becomes annoyingly slow and opens the door to ridicule from other truckers over the UHF radio.

Power and Off-Road modes, on the other hand, are very similar. Both modes permit the engine speed to rise higher than the torque-focused standard mode when making gearshifts. By using more power, in theory, reduces the number of shifts. Shifts are also faster in both these modes, either to speed progress or to minimise loss of traction, but consequently, the trade-off is fuel economy.

Smart Eco-roll
By early 2014 trucks built with Opticruise and integrated SAP also included the newly introduced eco-roll function. However, Opticruise will not always disengage the drivetrain going down every hill because when the truck is coasting downhill in gear, fuel delivery to the injectors is cut off; however, you still have driveline drag. On the other hand, using eco-roll eliminates driveline drag when the transmission shifts into neutral, but the engine requires fuel to keep it idling. Depending on the engine specification, fuel consumption at idle is 1.5 to 2.0 litres an hour. So Opticruise looks at the difference between the driveline drag losses and the fuel used with eco-roll, then calculates which approach uses less fuel. Scania estimated that eco-roll could generate fuel savings of up to two per cent in hilly terrain.

Shifting into the Next Decade
The current Opticruise transmission has served Scania operators for over two decades and recently received a significant design overhaul. In fact, the only thing that carried over from the older model is the name; "Opticruise". The G33-CM gearbox is an entirely new transmission.

At the launch, Scania said it is a colossal undertaking developing an entirely new gearbox range, especially when you will ultimately outperform what is already an industry benchmark. Consequently, the new Scania Opticruise gearbox range has no parts in common with the existing gearbox range.

"The design team's assignment was to develop gearboxes that could handle all the diverse demands of the next decade," Jimmy Larsson, Senior Manager, Head of Gearbox Development, Scania R&D, said. "Especially with fuel consumption, drivability, reliability and sustainability," "Furthermore, truck combinations with high GCMs can utilise fast axle gearing while still achieving the desired start-ability."

"Scania has an enduring tradition of offering powertrains with high torque, low engine RPM as key elements for achieving low fuel consumption," Lasson continued. "If a suitable cruising speed can be maintained at around, or just above, 1050 RPM, this will definitely save fuel. Up until recently, a typical long-distance truck operated on 1400 RPM. Scania's new gearbox range has a remarkably more comprehensive gear ratio spread with a genuine overdrive gear on top and can efficiently handle low and high revs.

Fuel-saving capability is a prominent feature with these new gearboxes, which is why Scania engineers focussed on reducing internal friction. Their intended target was reached, with internal losses reduced by no less than 50 per cent. This reduction was accomplished through polishing some of the gears, using low viscosity MTF oil and by relocating the lion's share of the oil into a separate, dry sump-like part on top of the gearbox. Subsequently, lowering the oil level in the transmission, in turn, lessens internal oil splash because the gears are not continuously covered in oil (imagine a water wheel). In addition, certain cog areas are vulnerable to hard-wearing when absorbing force. Spray pipes supply these cogs with extra oil for increased cooling and lubrication.

> **The new transmissions are considerably shorter than the most common of the older Scania gearboxes like the GRS905.**

The first release in the new Opticrusie transmission range, G33CM, is over 60 kg lighter than the current gearboxes, primarily due to the all-aluminium housings and somewhat smaller overall dimensions. Another significant achievement is reduced noise, an essential requirement for achieving future regulations. As a result, the average noise curtailment is up to 3.5 dB, quite a considerable drop considering that the dB scale is logarithmic.

The new transmissions are considerably shorter than the most common of the older Scania gearboxes like the GRS905. In addition, using only two synchronisers (compared to seven in the previous version) between high and low range split, the new

Above: Tomas Selling – Expert Engineer Transmission Development, explains the features of the new G33-CM Transmission at the launch.

gearboxes are shorter and sturdier, with shafts capable of handling far more torque. Subsequently, this enables opportunities to use gears with slightly wider cogs that can handle more load and are more durable.

However, removing synchronisers now places higher demands on the gearbox management system and the overall gear-shifting strategy. Consequently, all the electronic systems are new and manage the pneumatic actuators and the shaft brakes (three in total) that are instrumental for swift, smooth and accurate gearshifts.

Scania's engineers embraced a new approach to reversing. In most traditional gearboxes, going in reverse entails letting a separate cog wheel rotate the mainshaft in the opposite direction. By contrast, in the new Scania Opticrusie range, they employ a planetary engagement at the output shaft instead, and reversing is activated by locking up the planetary wheel carrier. This solution now provides the flexibility to use any of the eight gear ratios in the main box for reversing at speeds up to 54 km/h. This feature is undoubtedly valuable when, for instance, tip trucks reverse for long distances (such as at tunnel construction sites) or sugar cane haul-out applications.

Subsequently, oil change intervals are now greatly improved due to higher precision and the addition of larger oil filters and high-quality oil.

Needless to say, no truck gearbox range would be worth mentioning without also citing its Power Take-Off (PTO) capabilities. Scania's new Opticrusie range comes with an abundance of newly developed and clever PTO solutions to fulfil any number of advanced PTO needs, regardless of application.

In fact, a broad raft of nine different PTOs will be available, characterised by increased performance, greater flexibility via modularity and fewer drag losses. The EG PTOs are now directly driven by the layshaft and are pressure-lubricated by the gearbox. In addition, the new interface on the gearbox with a lubrication port means that they can power heavier equipment such as hydraulic pumps used for live bottom trailer discharge, truck-mounted cranes or walking floor operation.

If the engine speed of 1,050 RPM to 1,150 RPM is maintained while cruising, significant fuel is saved compared to much higher revving drivetrain configurations.

The combination of the high torque from the new Scania engines and the broader spread of total ratios in the gearbox make this achievable. The new gearbox also features an overdrive gear to maintain the lower engine speed level without compromising drivability. Engine-derived fuel savings in the region of 2 per cent are expected, resulting from re¬duced internal friction, higher compression ratios, improved after-treatment-systems and a new Engine Management System (EMS).

(*At the time of writing*). Operators covering 150,000kms per year can expect fuel savings of 3,000 – 4,000 litres per year, according to Scania's executive vice president Alexander Vlaskamp.

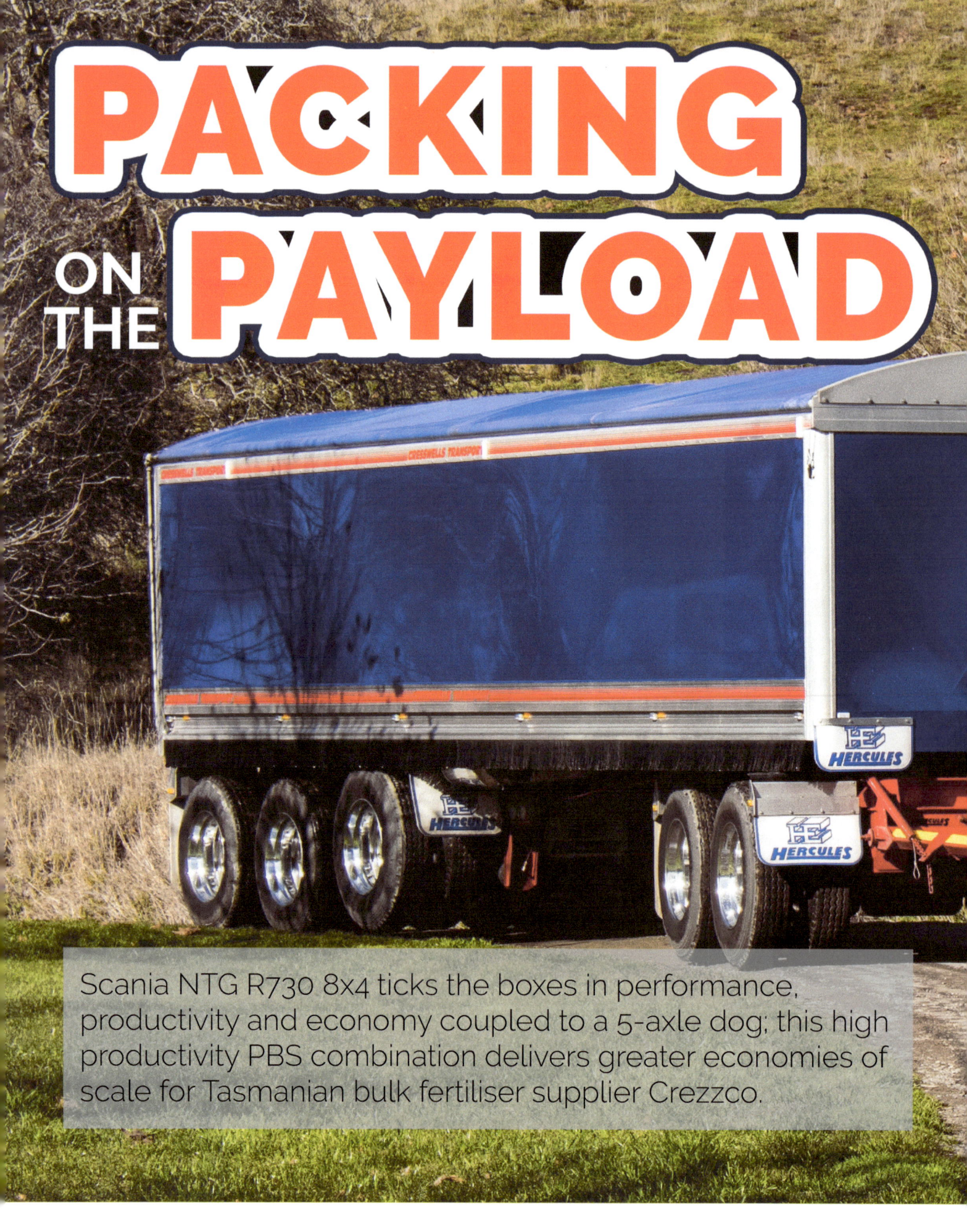

PACKING ON THE PAYLOAD

Scania NTG R730 8x4 ticks the boxes in performance, productivity and economy coupled to a 5-axle dog; this high productivity PBS combination delivers greater economies of scale for Tasmanian bulk fertiliser supplier Crezzco.

The sun was desperately trying to pierce through the thick blanket of fog that lingered well into the morning in the sleepy Meander Valley town of Deloraine in northern Tasmania. The serene stillness was slowly broken by the deep throb of the approaching Scania V8 in Crezzco's new R730 8x4. Moments later, owner Tony Creswell pulled the PBS combination onto the weighbridge and stepped down from the warm cabin.

"It's a bit fresh this morning," Tony said, introducing himself. "It's the 44.5-tonne payload that is impressing me," he smiled as he climbed back into the cabin.

Crezzco may well be a small family company that commenced operation back in the early seventies. However, through diversification, the business now operates several quarries, mines dolomite, has a concrete batch plant and is a primary carrier and distributor of Pivot fertiliser in the state.

Their truck and the earthmoving fleet are equally diverse, with carefully specified equipment to deliver the business's most economical outcome.

Despite freight rates almost remaining static for the last quarter century, Tony Creswell believes that adopting new technologies and specifying components according to need rather than tradition will lead to higher profits for the bulk haulage side of their operation.

Tony approaches new truck specifying with the sharpened pencil of an accountant. Combining a broad knowledge of the transport industry with an understanding of their customer needs and consideration for future regulations, he configures his trucks and trailers to safeguard the highest interests of his company.

"Maximising our equipment to the limit is one of our prime focuses now. This Scania Scania NTG R730 8x4, complete with the tipper combination, provides approximately a 0.72 tonne/kilometre payload advantage over some other vehicles we investigated. While that doesn't sound like much when you say it quickly, at the end of the month, all those point sevens add up," explained Tony. "As I said earlier, it is here on the weighbridge where it counts."

This new Scania's primary role is to haul dolomite from their Eddy Creek Quarry, located deep in the steep, rugged mountains southwest of Huonville that borders the "Huon and Florentine Valleys". It's an area with a long history of contention between forestry operations and environmental groups. Yet it is here that the tallest flowering plants in the world thrive – the Eucalyptus Regnans – that regularly gain heights of 80 meters and more. In terms of tall trees, these Tasmanian Eucalyptus are second only to the coastal redwoods in California, USA, that grow more than 100 meters tall.

The naturally occurring dolomite Crezzco's Eddy Creek Quarry produce gets crushed onsite to form a fine powder used as a soil conditioning and pH neutralising agent. Dolomite is an economical way to increase soil pH in acidic soils and to raise the magnesium levels in deficient soils while also adding calcium to assist improve soil structure and increase the availability of other trace elements.

"Our dolomite has an effective neutralising value (ENV) of 80.92 per cent, which makes it a premium grade product," Tony explained.

Given the fragile environment this Scania has to operate, Tony insisted that it have the latest Euro-6 engine.

"It is all part of our commitment to deliver a sustainable transport future not just for our business but our customers as well," Tony said. "We expect a lot of things from this new R730 in terms of reducing trip times through performance and reliability and improved fuel economy to reduce the cents per tonne/kilometre to ensure our agricultural products are economically viable for the farmers."

In order to understand why Tony is so adamant about

Tony demonstrated how effective the 'manoeuvre' setting on the Opticruise stalk is by accurately reversing the five-axle dog trailer into a bay inside the fertiliser shed.

Scania: Trucking in Australia

reducing his production costs, we need to explore his market and customer base. At the time of writing, the average price a farmer in Tasmania receives for their milk is $0.46/litre, while the average cost of milk in the supermarket is $1.60/litre. So by the time the farmer has paid all the expenses associated with producing the milk, there are little funds left out of that $0.46/litre to purchase fertilisers like dolomite.

"On a good day, it's a four-hour trip down to our Eddy Creek Quarry, where we load the dolomite," Tony explained. "Then it's roughly four and half hours back. There are several extremely long steep climbs up out of the quarry and along the Huon Hwy into Hobart where that Scania V8 really gets to strut its stuff."

"On paper, the R730 Scania had some impressive features," Tony recalled. "The fact that the engine is making 500 horsepower down as low at 1000 RPM where it begins making its peak torque was one factor that ticked a box for me. Being able to deliver that sort of power and torque with the latest Euro-6 emission standards certainly helps us reduce our carbon footprint," he added.

Like Tony said, the industry-leading peak torque of 3500Nm begins at 1000RPM and continues through to 1400RPM, where the big-hearted 16.4-litre V8 punches out 522 kW, loosely translated that's almost 700 HP in old-school trucking lingo. So when it comes to driveability, there is no performance compromise with the Euro-6 V8. It delivers the goods all the way through the sweet spot range.

This V8 engine uses a blend of SCR and ERG to achieve its Euro-6 emission standards, which means there is virtually no increase in ad-blue usage compared to the Euro-5 variant of the engine.

"The Scania 4100D retarder is really an essential component for our application," Tony explained. "There are some exceptionally long steep descents on the southern part of this run, especially coming down the southern outlet into Hobart, where it is densely populated, and the decline ends right in the city's heart. The Scania retarder is extremely quiet, which means we can utilise it any time of the day without upsetting the locals, and that's a huge advantage."

The new Scania 4100D retarder mechanically 'clutches out' when not in use to minimise parasitic drag and can generate a maximum of 4,100 Nm (3024 lb-ft) of braking.

"I like the fact that the braking system can be set to hold speed on downhills like a cruise control simply with the press of the brake pedal," Tony explained. "It autonomously blends the foundation brakes with the retarder and exhaust brakes to achieve maximum braking efficiency," he added.

The Scania GRS0925R 14-Speed Overdrive with the Opticruise shift features a layshaft brake that enables faster gear shifts, compared to the older model transmission, for better driveability with almost seamless hill-climbing and continuous power delivery. The addition of the layshaft brake means there is a 45 per cent reduction in gear shift time. As a result, this gearbox is changing gears quicker than formula one driver Daniel Ricciardo can punch through his 6-speed box exiting turn sixteen onto the main straight of Albert Park.

But it's not all about high speed; at lower speeds, a 'manoeuvre' setting on the Opticruise stalk enables the truck to be positioned with ultimate precision. Tony demonstrated how this worked when he accurately reversed the 5-axle Hercules dog trailer inside the fertiliser shed.

This Scania NTG R730 8x4 has the front air suspension, which dispenses with the previous Panhard rod arrangement found on early 8x4 models. The repositioning of the front axle gives excellent control with much less wallowing and nodding compared to rival trucks. In addition, the steering gear for the second axle layout is installed lower in the chassis to aid bodybuilders. The shock absorber mounting for this axle is also revised, and no longer rises above the chassis rails.

Inside Scania's Flagship R730 cabin, Tony says a driver wants for nothing. It has all the creature comforts. He adds the dash layout is practical and easy to see at a glance, meaning he has more time to concentrate on the road.

"That fact that you can virtually operate this vehicle with your fingers through controls located on the steering wheel makes life easy," Tony said. "The controls on the door armrest also add to the ease of the operation of this truck. There is plenty of storage room inside too, not that we probably need the sleeper's features as we're home nearly every night, but it's handy to have all the same."

It's only early days for the new Scania NTG R730 8x4 with its Hercules 5-axle dog combo. Along with Tony's productivity gains from the unique combination, he concedes that given the current driver shortage, it is far easier to get a driver for this unit because they don't need a multi-combination licence to drive a truck and dog. Yet it delivers a payload compatible with a B-Double with more tyres on the ground.

"And that's another great thing about the new Scania; it has a lot of inbuilt smarts that keep it operating in the sweet spot all the time, including the active cruise with braking," Tony added. "For instance, if a driver was distracted and didn't notice a car pull in front of the truck and brake suddenly, the truck will automatically brake. It's that level of safety that really gives us owners peace of mind."

"As I said earlier, the R730 ticked all the boxes for us in terms of productivity, performance, economy and safety," Tony concluded. "For me, it's about delivering the biggest payload economically and safely. After all, where it counts is on the weighbridge."

TRUCK SPECIFICATIONS

Model:	Scania R730 8x4
Engine:	Scania DC16 730 16-Litre 8-Cylinder
Horsepower:	730 hp (537)kw @1900 RPM
Torque:	2581 lb/ft (3500Nm) @ 1000-1400 RPM
Gearbox:	Scania GRS0925R 14-Speed Overdrive
Gearbox shift:	Scania Opticruise
Retarder:	Scania 4100D (plus engine exhaust brake)
Alternator:	Scania 24V 150amp
Compressor:	Knorr 720CR, twin cyl, 800L/m
Propeller Shaft:	P604
Steering Box:	ZF 8098
Front Axles:	Scania AM640S-
Front Suspension:	Scania 2 x Air Bag (Low)
Rear Axles:	Scania AD400SA axle housings
Rear Axle Ratio:	3.42:1 with diff locks to both axles
Rear Suspension:	Scania 2 x Air Bag with roll bar
Brakes:	Knoor electronically controlled Disc brakes
Tyres:	Bridgestone 295/80R22.5
Safety:	EBS with integrated ABS and traction control
Wheelbase:	5150mm
Cab Tilt:	Electronic
Interior:	Premium with leatherette Black V8
Seats:	Premium driver's seat with armrests
Battery Box:	2x12V, 180-amp Chassis mount LH side
Fuel Tank:	1 x 600L L/H side
Adblue tank:	1 x 47L R/H side

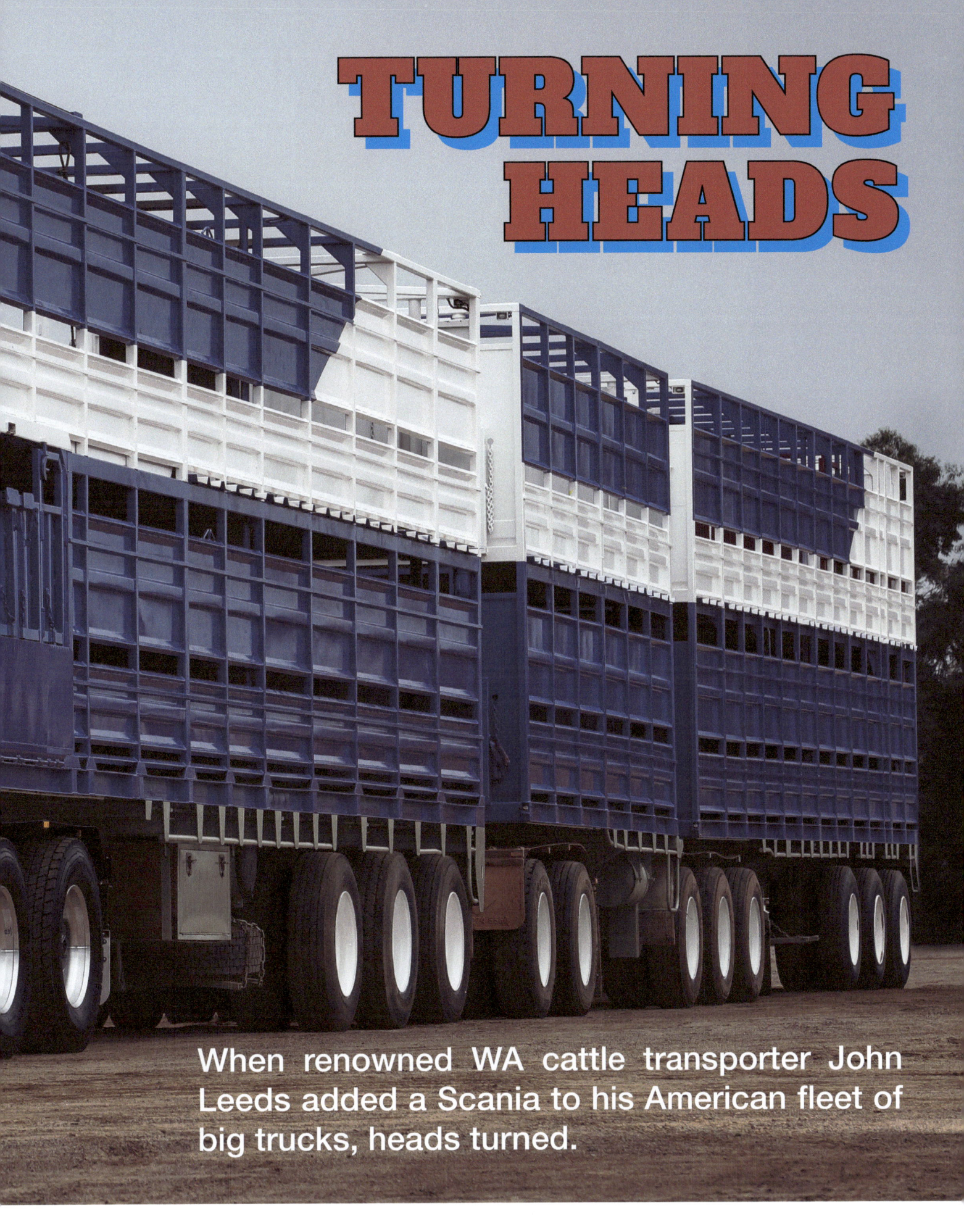

TURNING HEADS

When renowned WA cattle transporter John Leeds added a Scania to his American fleet of big trucks, heads turned.

Most of us need a compelling reason to break lifelong traditions. Leeds Cattle Transport patriarch John Leeds is no different. So when the Scania R 730 caught his eye, a lifelong tradition of owning American trucks came to an end.

Operating in heat and dust along the ravaged roads and bush tracks of the northern Pilbara region in Western Australia is a rigorous testing ground for any truck. Yet, at the time of writing, his first R 730, now six months old, has more than proven its worth.

John and his wife Pam started Leeds Cattle Transport with a single Dodge truck in Carnarvon in 1972, originally carting sheep but soon turned to cattle, and as the business grew, they moved to Pardoo Station at Port Headland from 1991 to 2005. In addition to the cattle transport business, based in Bullsbrook on the outskirts of Perth, there is also a live cattle holding depot and a farm.

It's a family-owned business that includes sons Justin and Matthew, who grew up around trucks and cattle. Sixty decks and twelve prime movers make up the Leeds fleet, and when not moving cattle between April and December, the downtime is used to carry out maintenance and put their tippers to work in the grain season. In a departure from his all-American fleet of 11 trucks, John explains the reason behind purchasing his first-ever Scania.

"I bought it because I wanted to see if the 730 horsepower was really there, and so far, I am pretty happy with it. We've used American trucks for a long time, and we know they do put out the horsepower, but up until now, I haven't had much experience with European trucks. But there's no doubt it (the Scania) has 730 horses," he said.

Over the year, each truck averages 200,000 km, operating mainly in the Port Headland, Carnarvon, and Meekathara triangle, along with regular trips to Perth. Road conditions are far from perfect;

Left: John Leeds and his faithful mate with his Scania R730 that is turning a few heads.

Above: John Leeds at the wheel of his Scania R 730 prime mover. In the background a row of the old brigade parked up.

"Sixty-five per cent of the roads we use are bitumen," says John, "with the rest of it pretty savage dirt; rough, corrugated and not very well maintained. They vary significantly in condition depending on how many trucks have used them before you get there.

"Although we don't go anywhere near them in the wet season because you can't operate then, this year has been quite wet, and we've had many hold-ups in the early part of the season," he added.

Perched on 60 wheels and with a gross weight of 130 tonnes, the Scania and its three-and-a-half trailers is longer than an Olympic swimming pool.
Keeping an eye on costs, John has noted Scania's fuel efficiency and tyre life.

"Fuel economy is a big issue for us," John explained. "And we didn't know whether the fuel economy was gonna' be any good until we got out on the road and started hauling our triple trailers. We noticed pretty quickly the fuel economy of the Scania was very good, proving to be about 0.2 litres per km better than the American motors.

"Another combination we pull is a B-double and dog, or five decks. We've found that set up is also getting exceptional economy. In fact, we are sending the Scania from Perth to Mount Isa with five decks to bring back a herd of cattle. We reckon it will probably do around 1.4 to 1.5 km/litre, and we don't see that sort of fuel economy from our other trucks.

"We're also finding the Scania is kind to its steer tyres, and after 100,000 km, they don't even have a mark on them," he says. "There's no sign of any misalignment or scrubbing, and the drive tyres are only about 40% worn after 100,000 km. What does most of the tyre damage are the roads themselves. The tyres could be wearing beautifully up to a point, and all of a sudden, you go down a couple of the roads we use, and they'll tear the hell out of them. But some of it goes back to the horsepower at the wheels and the load we are carrying," he says.

Operating in such a harsh, isolated environment means reliability is paramount, and though just six months old, the Scania has been trouble-free.

According to John, as an extra safeguard, Leeds trucks are serviced more often than recommended as the cost of a little extra oil and filters is nothing compared to being stuck on the side of the road waiting for a service vehicle. Or worse still, hoping the service truck can actually find them in the first place, given some of the isolated areas that Leeds operates in. Although Leeds had hired a Scania truck in the past, when one of its company trucks was off the road, the Scania Opticruise automated transmission was another first for John.

"I'm more than happy with it," he says. "The only problem I

had was putting my foot down and realising there is no clutch which is a bit funny," he laughs. "But I think they (Scania) have got that technology worked out. We've had some pretty heavy loads on it, and it doesn't seem to have any problems getting the job done."

As a leader in cattle transport, Leeds Transport is often the first to introduce new practices, technology, trucks and trailers. So when word got out down the bush telegraph that Leeds Transport was buying a Scania, many in the industry didn't believe it until they saw it painted up in the company colours on the road.

"Yeah, I've had a few remarks, and some didn't believe it until they saw it. All I can say is we made a decision to buy the Scania, and we certainly haven't regretted it."

According to John, given the experience Leeds Cattle Transport has enjoyed with their Scania so far, more could soon be joining the fleet.

"We are looking very closely at one right now, and if Scania is willing to work with us, they have a big future. We need trucks that will work in the bush, not just on the highways. We are talking with them about the spec for their mining trucks regarding bigger fuel tanks and a longer chassis, so they will suit what we and others in the industry do."

"Scania welcomes Leeds Cattle Transport to the Scania family," says Michael Berti, Regional Executive Manager at Scania WA. "Scania trucks are robust, powerful, and well-suited to cattle transport. "We already have several livestock industry operators in WA and around Australia using our vehicles, and globally Scania has a strong reputation in cattle transport. In fact, our smooth shifting transmissions give the cattle a more comfortable journey, which means they arrive at their destination in better condition and less stressed.

"We have regular dialogue with John and his team about the performance of the R 730 to optimise the specification further to suit what is an arduous application and deliver maximum uptime.

"Leed's Cattle Transport is renowned in the industry for delivering first time, every time, for their customers. Reliability is critical to John's business, and the Leed's fleet regularly goes to places that many other operators would consider off limits.

"In reality, Leed's R 730 works in conditions more akin to a mining application. As John says, we are borrowing features from our ultra-heavy duty mining prime movers as we refine the specification for what will hopefully be the next Scania in this customer fleet.

"We are delighted to have John Leeds as a customer of Scania, and he joins a growing list of long-standing operators of American trucks who have decided to give Scania ago and have found to their delight that our trucks do what we say and help them deliver enhanced profitability," Michael says.

MOVIN' ON
R730

Scania: Trucking in Australia

Western Australia is as varied as it is vast. In the south-eastern corner lies the regional centre of Esperance; a mix of a seaside town, farming town, bulk tanker-handling import and export terminal, as well as the exit point for a chunk of the state's huge iron ore reserves.

Blessed with beautiful beaches, balmy weather (mostly), and boundless plains, the fruits of the colonial settlement have resulted in widespread farming of commodity crops, grazing and even the planting of commercial forestry, all the while harbouring an active mining sector for nickel and iron ore.

The busy port terminal hosts oil tanker deliveries. At the same time, bulk grain and iron ore carriers queue up within the sweeping bay, waiting their turn to nuzzle the conveyor belts that spill out renewable products of wheat, barley, canola, and non-renewable supplies of unprocessed mineral wealth.

In essence, Esperance has the perfect trifecta to deliver stability. The three legs of the economic stool that support the community of 15,000 souls are tourism and mineral and agricultural exports. If one is slow, the other may step in to carry more or the load.

Esperance is progressive, too, being the first to establish a wind farm in WA. Its 16 turbines provide up to 30 per cent of the town's power requirement. However, sustained by decent rains during the year, the farmers' initial glee at the size and quality of the crop may have dulled slightly as late rains arrived in early November.

But at an estimated three million tonnes, it'll be a record year in terms of volume, bringing smiles to the faces of most of the town, from the shipping agents to the bankers, the farm machinery suppliers and the transport subbies.

This year's iron ore exports will amount to 11 million tonnes, though the daily transfer of one million litres of diesel from the port to the mines to run power generation has ceased since they became more self-sufficient.

As the roads hum with B-Doubles and C-Trains whistling up and down the well-made single-lane byways in tidy but modest premises close by the main drag, Michael Harding, owner of Esperance Freight Lines can pause to reflect on the state of the local economy.

"Esperance Freight Lines will always rely on agriculture, but we'll never put all our eggs in that basket," he says. "This harvest, we have 38 road trains (including sub-contractors trucks) on the road moving grain.

In fact, as Esperance, the town, rests securely on a diversified approach to economic survival, Esperance Freight Lines has similarly spread its risk across

supermarket delivery (a refrigerated B-Trailer and dry food B-Trailer arrive daily from Perth for two national chain retailers), general freight, seasonal agricultural transport to silos and the port, as well as Nickel Concentrate transfers ship side and Sulphur transport from the wharf to mine. The spread across the industries gives protection against unseasonal performance or the cyclical boom-bust tempo of commodities exports.

Michael Harding grew up around trucks, worked for his father, and then for – and later with – his brother-in-law in Esperance Freight Lines as Operations Manager before buying out the company with Colin Danks in 2003. Then in 2010, Michael and his partner, Katherine Ann, became the sole owners of the business.

"We started with five trucks and 20 trailers in 2003, and now we're up to more than 70 trucks and 300 trailers. We move anything except livestock," Michael says. "Early on, Dad had a Scania on a fruit and veg run. Today we have around 40 Scanias, and a mix of American and European brands make up the rest of the fleet.

"Overall, we're comfortable with Scania, and they don't break down. We know that they are good on fuel if you drive them properly. Most modern trucks are good on fuel, but the driver needs to understand the truck. The driver is key to fuel use," Michael says.

"Around 80 per cent of our drivers have been with us more than five years, and we have taught the older guys to love the auto (Opticruise) gearbox. We had one driver who was very focused on a manual gearbox. However, we sent him out on a drive in the Opticruise, and he called back after only 38 km, saying how much he loved it and didn't want to get out of the truck.

> **Michael is one of a diminishing number of transport professionals who continue to run the business from the coalface.**

Above: On the farm, grain is loaded into the trailers with a screw auger from mobile storage bins.

Below: Tipping off one load of grain that will make up the many loads required to achieve the total estimated 1.5 million tonnes of grain EPL will shift this season.

Scania: Trucking in Australia

"The Scanias are comfortable, quiet in the cab and reliable. When driven properly, we get good fuel. We rely on our drivers to drive well to get good fuel results. Fuel and wages are the highest costs of our business," he reveals.

For a transport operator with close to 80 trucks and 300 trailers in the inventory, three yards in Esperance and further depots in Albany, Geraldton, Kalgoorlie, Perth, Ravensthorpe and Welshpool, you'd be forgiven for thinking Michael would be welded to the desk in his spacious, light and airy office drowning in spreadsheets. But the truth is far different.

Never happier than behind the wheel on the road, Michael is one of a diminishing number of transport professionals who continue to run the business from the coalface.

"I drive an R 730. I often need to be driving full time to get the job done," he explains. "Because I have a good crew behind me, I can be behind the wheel driving (while they run the business). The secret to the success of Esperance Freight Lines has been the relationships we have built up over the years with the people we do business with," Michael adds.

"Our customers know if they want to talk to the boss, they just pick up the phone and talk to me. They don't go through layers of management. They like that direct access, which means we can get the job done or the issue sorted out," he says.

At the time of writing, Michael and Katherine Ann have a tight-knit management team with their fingers firmly on the pulse of every vehicle and every job. That team includes; Milton Valli, company Financial Controller – soon to be heading for semi-retirement after eight years with the company but staying on as company secretary. Priyanka Shivran, the company accountant. Andy Giles, in charge of general freight, and Eric Carter, who runs the workshop. That's no mean feat.

The search for efficiency has driven the adoption of Scania's 8x4 Twin Steer configuration for his pocket road trains and C-trains (an A-trailer and two B-doubles).

The 8x4 chassis has been teamed with the Scania King of the Road R 730 V8 engine to provide effortless pulling power all the way to 115 tonnes gross under the harvest concession, day-in, day-out, amounting to around 78 tonnes of payload per trip.

Esperance Freight Lines purchased two Scania R 730 8x4 in 2014 and 2 more in 2015, all of which were hitched to new Howard Porter bulk grain tippers, and the combination measure 36.5 m in length. Weigh scales on all axles enhance the all-around airbag suspension, which is helpful for combinations running exceptionally heavy loads.

"When I saw the R 730, I thought we'd give it a go," Michael says. "We use the R 730 8x4 for bulk grain and fertiliser while the R 620s are used on general freight and can go anywhere and do anything."

The company transports daily from Perth all of the dry and refrigerated food for Woolworths and IGA in Esperance, using Scania B-doubles. One trailer is a refrigerated pan, and the others a Vawdrey tautliner. These trucks cover 1.0 million km in 5 years on this route. The trucks can stop halfway to Perth, and the drivers switch over, returning to Esperance to be able to sleep at home.

The Esperance Freight Lines fleet includes every V8 engine output range variant: 500, 560, 620 and 730 hp engines performing various roles.

A bonneted T143 V8 Scania Topline is tucked away in the yard, which obviously is too well loved to be moved on. At the same time, another early Scania can still be pressed into service come the need, despite seeing more than 1.6 m km under its wheels to date.

During the harvest period, there won't be any spare trailers left resting up in the yards. However, during our visit in November, amid an unseasonably chilly and wet spell, farmers were forced to suspend loading and transporting as the crop's moisture content was too great for the CBH silos to accept.

For some, the solution is a trip to the drying yards and then off to one of the 11 CBH receiving yards in the district, but others withheld deliveries until the sun returned to dry out the crop naturally.

We'll aim to cart around half of the three million tonnes of grain from Esperance region this harvest," says Milton Valli, and about one-third of this amount out of Geraldton. We only deliver to CBH. While some of the grain gets used domestically, much is exported worldwide to China, the Middle East, Japan and Europe," he adds.

In addition to the dry and refrigerated food and bulk grain transport, the business also runs a fleet of five trucks 24/7 towing three trailers of close to 80 tonnes of sulphur from the port to the nickel mines, where it is used as an integral part of the extraction process.

The payload is large and the demand high, so the trucks barely rest, completing four round trips each day, and again Scania trucks play a formidable role in keeping this side of the business running.

We'll cover, on average, around 180,000 kilometres per year on each truck, but some do more than others. So, for example, the sulphur delivery trucks will do 400,000 km, and the Perth food freight trucks will do 350,000 km," Michael adds.

According to Trevor Furnace – another long-serving staffer who readily returns to the fold from semi-retirement to his old role as Operations Manager to help Michael out – the strength of the Esperance Freight Lines and Scania relationship is reliability and performance.

"Michael's always leaned towards Scania, though we have tried other trucks. But we're back with Scania now. We know they can do the job. The first 18 trucks Michael put into the fleet were Scania. We run the newer trucks on the Scania Maintenance and Repair contracts," he informs.

"The Maintenance and Repair contracts mean I can deal with fixed costs," Michael adds. "I know what my trucks will cost me, and I run them on operating leases, turning them over after four or five years. I 'don't want to own 70 trucks outright, but we buy the trailers. They work for longer, and there'll always be a buyer for a trailer if we need to move them on.

Esperance Freight Lines provides a good snapshot of a valued Scania customer partnership," says Keith Berwick, New Truck Account Manager for Scania WA, based out of Kewdale, Perth Branch.

Scania: Trucking in Australia

"They cart big loads in three trailers, and they have trucks on the roads all day and all night in some cases. Reliability, durability and after-sales backup are the keys to their uptime, as is the Maintenance and Repair programme we have running with our dealer Kip & Steve Mechanical Repairs, based close by in the town.

"We have had a long and close relationship with the business over several years," Keith says. "They trust us to find them a tailored solution, such as the airbag-equipped R730 8x4 that allows them to go up to 115-tonnes in safety, but also with fuel efficiency and driver comfort as well," Keith says.

"You couldn't get a better endorsement of the product than by having the boss drive the Scania flagship because he wants to drive, not just because he has to.

Driver's View

Driving the Scania R730 V8 8x4 pulling two B-Trailers, the engine's additional power over the previous R 620 really makes itself felt, says Rob Mellor, a driver with Esperance Freight Lines.

Speaking among the grain storage on Jake and Clara Graham's sprawling farm with Wittenoom Hills, 80 km outside Esperance, Rob says the airbag suspension all around gives the truck a very steady and solid feel on the road.

"The ride is outstanding, and the trailers are very stable," he says. "we're pulling 115-tonne gross, so around 78-tonne payload. My biggest load was 80 tonnes for 117,200 kg gross, with only a few hundred to spare under the concession. That was barley. It's heavier than wheat.
Rob's been with Esperance Freight Lines for around 18 months after 50 years of driving trucks, and the Kiwi native still enjoys driving road trains.

"I drove my first road train in 1987 in Australia," he reveals. "And I had a few years in the mines. But the R730 takes comfort and grunt into another class," he adds.

"On some 8x4s, you'd say you'd hit the same bump twice, but in the Scania, you don't even feel it once. The steering is not any heavier than a single steer, though it doesn't self-centre as easily as single front axle trucks, so you have to be ready for it.

"I like the Scania cab, and you can see out very well Rob says.

Scania: Trucking in Australia 117

Clean & Green

And, frequently seen – Tasmania's first Road Train.

Scrap metal recycler Recycal is employing Scania's onboard technology systems to push high productivity vehicle utilisation to the next level, introducing a 35-meter Type-1 Road Train high productivity vehicle running HML mass. The first of its kind in Tasmania.

Most of Launceston was still sleeping. When Kym Lawrence climbed up into the cabin of the Scania R620 coupled up to two purpose-built Tefco trailers and triaxle dolly a little before 5 am on a cold frosty morning. Kym turned the key, and the 16-litre V-8 Scania engine purred into life. He wasted little time walking around the rig in the chilled morning air, checking lights and tyres.

"We're good to go," he informed, climbing back into the truck.

This return journey to Recycal's southern depot at Brighton on the northern outskirts of Hobart in the state's south with the 35-meter Type-1 Road Train is the culmination of over 12 months of dedicated work behind the scenes. Understandably, the approval process for a combination of this size requires a lengthy list of criteria gets achieved before consideration for any approval to be granted.
The raison d'etre behind the development of this combination for Recycal was not only to reduce transport costs between their Hobart and Launceston facilities but further to reduce their transport movements on the road network and consequently reduce emissions per tonnes of freight transported.

"This combination will primarily transport all the pressings and Heavy Melting Steel (HMS steel) from our Hobart collection centre through to Launceston, where we have a 15-acre purpose-built recycling facility," said Rob Massey, Launceston Operations Manager.

"Here at Recycal (Tasmania), we are in a unique position because of the strategic partnership we have with local foundry Castings Tasmania," Rob informed. "It's probably one of the oldest companies in the country that trace its routes back to meagre beginnings in 1833 trading as Johns Perry Castings. We're proud the foundry has maintained a reputation for quality castings through a range of ownerships over almost two centuries of continuous operation, somewhat of a record in Australian terms. We'd developed an alliance with the business in 2016, and by December 2019, Castings Tasmania became part of the Recycal Group."

"We (Recycal) now work closely with our sister company Castings Tasmania to supply quality steel needed for the foundry," Rob explained. "At our Launceston facility, we utilise the latest portable X-Ray guns that can sort metal in various grades so we can take advantage of the range of alloys, matching the best scrap to the right castings. It's a strategic alliance we hope will ensure that local scrap arisings, local labour and know-how will guarantee quality castings continue to be made here in Tasmania for the foreseeable future."

"But to make that happen, we need to get the raw

> **"We have been utilising the Scania tracking and reporting system for some time now to help improve our drivers"**

materials into the factory at the lowest cost possible," Rob continued. "Every drop of fuel burned in each machine's engine that handles our materials counts. It all equates to cost per tonne of payload."

The combination is rated for up to 92-tonnes GCM. "However, we are currently capped at 85-tonnes for the moment because on a few bridges along the route," Rob informed. "But we're confident we'll operate at full payload capacity soon after all upgrades get completed."

Future-proofing their business with vehicle assets like the Scania R620 V8 allows Recycle to develop and grow vehicle combinations to meet their ever-changing transport requirements better.

The low-revving DC16 Scania V8 engine is ideally suited to multi-combination applications. This unit is rated at 620 HP (456 kW at 1900 RPM punching out an impressive 2213 lb-ft (3000 Nm) between 950 – 1400 rpm. Its abundance of power enables it to economically haul the 35-meter type-1 road train.

However, at Recycle they have a holistic approach to transport operation that includes environmental impact, safety and road-user courtesy which are all non-negotiable standards in the business. In addition, the company embraces Scania's vehicle and driver monitoring services to help keep their drivers focused on their job, their operating environment and driving efficiencies.

"We have been utilising the Scania tracking and reporting system for some time now to help improve our drivers' habits," Rob explained.

"The system assists in creating a good driving culture, and it's pleasing to see our guys compare themselves

"The Scania system is like a driver's digital resume," Rob said. "If a driver applies for a job and shows that their driver score is consistently high, they'll be sort after by many transport businesses."

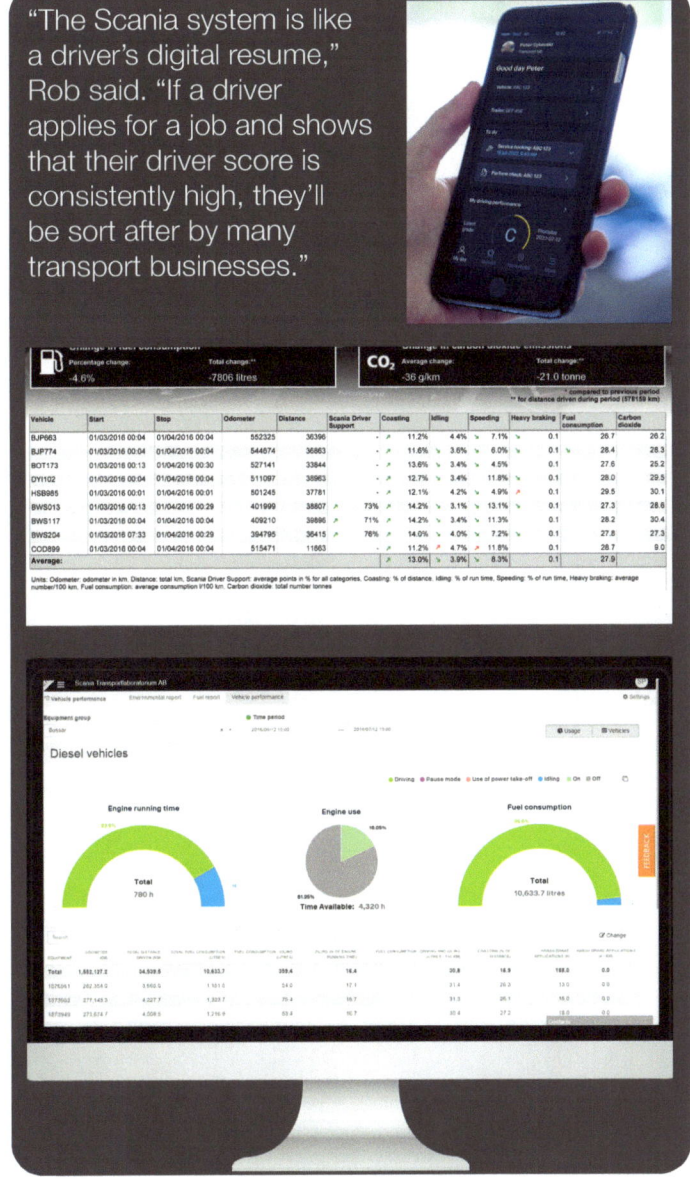

Scania: Trucking in Australia

Left: Driver, Kym Lawrence says the standard inbuilt safety features and technology in the Scania greatly assisted the company getting the permits to run Tasmania's first 35-meter road train.
Below Left: Loading scrap metal in Hobart for recycling in Launceston in the north of the island state.
2nd from Bottom: A forklift with a broom sweeps the floor area around the truck to minimise punctures and maintain a safe work environment.
Bottom Left: Kym weighs each load on the weighbridge even though the vehicle is equipped with on board scales.

against each other," Rob revealed. "I often get calls from drivers when someone else is driving their truck, to say 'just want you to know that so-and-so is driving my truck today so that their score is not misinterpreted by us when someone else is driving their truck."

Rob believes that Scania's driver monitoring system assists drivers to perform better because there is full tracking and accountability for each driver.

"The Scania system is like a driver's digital resume," Rob said. "If a driver applies for a job and shows that their driver score is consistently high, they'll be sort after by many transport businesses."

"Truth be told, now and then, a little internal competition is always healthy," he added with a smile.

Recycle embraced Scania's complete repair and maintenance contract service. This gives the business full transparency of running costs with predictable month-by-month costs. The servicing work is carried out at Scania's branches authorised service agents in Tasmania. But as a bonus, consistent high driver scores give Recycle a reduction in cents per kilometre from their R&M contract.

Rob admits that some drivers focus on achieving exceptionally high scores more than others.

"it is pleasing to see the majority of our drivers all strive to average 90-95%, although we are even seeing scores of 100% coming through from time to time. A handful of drivers are less focused, but it gives us a point of conversation to have with them. If we have ten vehicles all doing the same work, and there is a big difference in scores, then we need to work out why this is happening. We understand there are many factors, from traffic congestion on the day or too much idling to a driver merely having a bad day, and they're a bit harsher on the brakes and acceleration.

"But that is addressed through driver training, and Scania's driver training has been good too," Rob said.

TRUCK SPECIFICATIONS

Model:	Scania R620
Engine:	Scania DC16 620 16-Litre V8
Horsepower:	620 hp (456)kw @1900 RPM
Torque:	2213 lb/ft (3000Nm) @ 950-1400 RPM
Gearbox:	Scania GRS0905R 12-speed OD + 2 crawlers
Retarder:	Scania R4100
PTO:	Rear EG652P
Alternator:	Scania 24V 150amp
Compressor:	Knorr 720, twin cylinder, 800 L/min with air dryer
Front Axles:	Scania AM 740
Front Suspension:	Parabolic 7,200kg with anti-roll bar
Rear Axles:	Scania ADA 1501P axle housings with RBP 835 gears
Rear Axle Ratio:	3.96 with diff locks to both axles
Rear Suspension:	Scania 4-Bag, 21,000 kg
Brakes:	Scania electronically controlled disc brakes
Safety:	EBS with integrated ABS and traction control
Interior:	Velour Trim
Seats:	Premium driver's seat with armrests
Bumper:	Alloy
Battery Box:	2x12V, 180 amp rear chassis mount
Fuel Tank:	1 x 400L R/H side
Adblue tank:	1 x 70L L/H side

Trailers

Make:	Tefco
Model:	Road Train Combination – 160m cube
Body:	Hardox 450 Wear Resistant Steel
Tailgate:	Side single hinge gate
Suspension:	Hendrickson Intraax
Brakes:	Knorr-Bremse EBS with TIMS module
Hoist:	ROC – dual ported
Wheels:	Alloy 10-stud 335PCD
Lights:	LED

Scania: Trucking in Australia

"As we get new drivers, we want to get them trained, learn how to get the best from the vehicles, and fully understand the technology on board. So Scania, assist us with that too."

"From a driver's perspective, the Scania is a very comfortable truck to drive," driver Kym Lawrence explained. "They are well appointed and even come with a fridge. It's amazing how a few little creature comforts make the day much more enjoyable."

"Here on the Midland highway, there are few steep hills, and the Scania retarder is a great asset," Kym added. "When you operate the truck, and it's driven properly, the results are fantastic, and I hardly need to use the foot brakes at all, which is a significant saving on wear and tear in this sort of terrain."

"I'm impressed with Scania's Lane Departure Warning and Adaptive Cruise Control, especially with the topography reading Active Prediction is great for the hilly areas. But the Downhill Speed Control certainly gets a thorough workout on this run. It won't let you speed," Kym says. "That's important too because my speed is monitored not just by us but by State Growth, who issued the permit for combination.

"It is a harsh working environment we operate in, and our vehicles need to stand up to the job, and we work hard to keep them looking like new," Kym explained.

"It's part of our brand image," he added. "I washed this before I went home last night, but even though we haven't made it through Campbell Town and it's drizzling, it still looks reasonably clean.

For the Recycle Group, the efficiency of their transport operation is not just paramount to delivering a healthy bottom line to their transport business. It is essential to ensure the continued viability of their casting operation by supplying raw materials at a cost that enables them to compete with the world market. And thanks to Scania's onboard telematics electronic monitoring and mentoring systems, Recycal has introduced a new level of consciousness among its drivers to boost operational efficiency and increase productivity with expanded vehicle utilisation.

Scania: Trucking in Australia

125

SCANIA MINING TRUCKS

In Australia, most mine sites tend to lie where it's hot, dam hot, in the remotest regions of the continent. Then there's the dust and the long deep corrugated roads. And finally, the enormous loads.

These are the stories of some unique Scania mine spec trucks hauling more than just precious ore from the coal face to the processing plant.

Hub Reduction Diffs Explained

Regular readers would recall that we've reported on several tri-drive units operating in high productivity heavy road train applications over the last few years. Truth be told, the site of a tri-drive or "tridem" road train with four to six trailers in tow is indeed an impressive sight. Their daily payloads undoubtedly would have made the record books not so long back. But is this pioneering a new road train era? Some think so.

But in the minefields of Western Australia, one Scania truck utilises a different approach to the traditional tri-drive concept. They employ a bogie drive heavy-duty hub reduction rear axle set with a lazy tag axle to make up the tri-group. So, we asked, what are the benefits and how does the hub reduction rear axle work?

A decade or so back, increased weight limits on tri-axle groups in Western Australia sparked the tri-drive revolution for road-going trucks, which saw engineers scribbling frantically over their drawing machines to get a new product to market. Many operators questioned how hard it could be to lengthen a chassis and slot in an extra drive axle. Numerous company GMs, Accountants and Marketing Managers agreed. Yet back down in the engineering department, engineers were busier than ants at the Moomba day picnic. The larger payloads demanded increased power to propel the heavier loads. In addition, vastly different gearing and heavier-duty drivelines were needed to meet stringent gradeability and startability requirements.

If you're as old as me by some chance, you'll have probably played with an old manually driven Meccano set as a kid. On the other hand, if you're my son's age and like machinery and trucks, the Meccano set you'd probably have used would be a little more modern and include electric motors and remote control. Trucks are very much like a Meccano set. Scania engineers know this too well and have designed Scania components to integrate, with one another, much like a Meccano set. Thankfully for truck specialists, like Scania's Mining and Resources Division General Manager Robert Taylor, when Qube enquired about a prime mover to haul one of their latest Super-Quad, Robert merely searched through Scania's extensive components catalogue. He selected the parts that best suited the design application to produce the R730 10x8 Super-Quad road train.

To better understand how this process works, take a look at a few of the options in Scania's XT range of trucks. When an operator purchases their new Scania, they first choose one of five models and then select their preferred cabin, High, Normal or Low. Then, based on their application, they choose an axle configuration, an engine, a transmission, and so on until they have a truck that meets their needs, much like a Meccano set.

But let's rewind the clock a few years. Those original first tri-drive units operating in remote regions generated overwhelming success.

But let's rewind the clock a few years. Those original first tri-drive units operating in remote regions generated overwhelming success. They indeed delivered significant efficiencies as over-the-road movers of large quantities of bulk product, and favourable acceptance from local regulatory bodies paved the way for their broader spread utilisation.

However, the ongoing success of heavy-duty tri-drive units eventually paved the way for a more fuel-efficient tandem drive lazy axle configuration that afforded the same axle group weight limits as a tri-drive. Yet this new tri-group variant offered additional benefits such as fuel saving because the power required to drive two differentials is far less than needed to drive three. Furthermore, there's a slight payload advantage as the lazy axle option is lighter than a driving axle.

Western Australia's AMMS accreditation allows far more generous axle weight allowances than the eastern states' operators are afforded under NHVR regulations. Consequently, WA is the largest user of tridem prime movers in the country. When commissioned, Qube's Scania R730 10x8 and its set of PBS super-quad trailers haul iron ore with an impressive 220 tonnes gross train weight.

The 10x8 Scania hauls bulk iron ore around the clock from various mine sites to the shipping terminal at Port Hedland.

"This Scania operates around the clock six-and-a-half days a week," Todd Emmert, Director of Qube Bulk, said. "Some of the mine sites are 450 km from the port. We anticipate our Scania trucks to clock up close to one million kilometres in the first three years of their working life here in the Pilbara.

"One of the benefits of the higher payload is ultimately reducing the number of truck movements on a given

Above Left: Qube's Don White in front of the 10x8.
Above Right: The addition of the lazy axle behind the drive bogies makes this the longest Scania yet in Australia, with a 4.7m axle distance.
Below: The planetary gears in the Hub Reduction wheel end.
Bottom: The lubrication diagram of the planetary gears shows how oil flow changes with the vehicle speed.

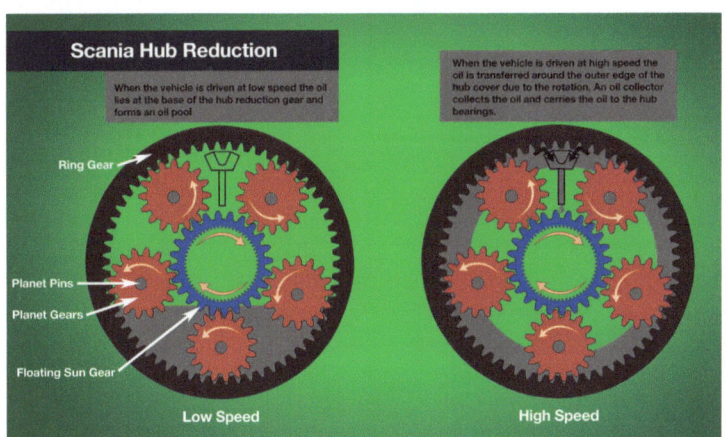

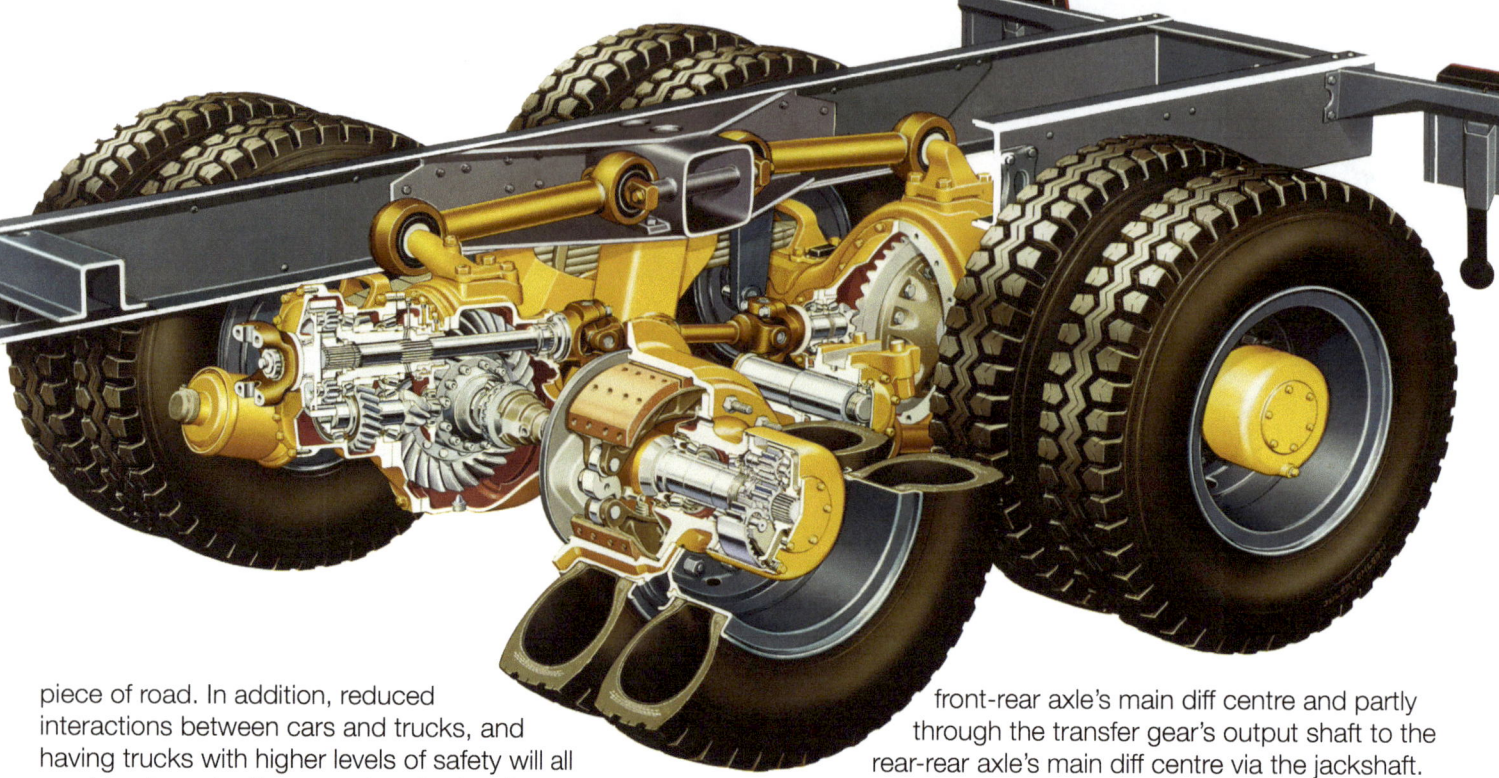

piece of road. In addition, reduced interactions between cars and trucks, and having trucks with higher levels of safety will all combine to make these roads safer for all road users," Todd added.

"Scania has accumulated abundant mining services experience worldwide, particularly in the harsh, remote Australian outback," Robert Taylor continued. "We continue to work closely with many mining operators to offer reliable products with the flexibility to take advantage of payload improvements under PBS.

"What we have learned has improved our customers' product and operational experience, and we are confident that even one million arduous km of operation for this configuration will not trouble this very impressive V8-powered 10x8 prime mover," Robert smiled.

Hub Reduction

One advantage of a hub reduction or planetary drive rear axle is that the input torque gets reduced twice. First in the differential centre and then through the planetary drive wheel ends. Another advantage, especially for trucks like this Scania that operate out of mines and quarries, is the high ground clearance. In the case of the Scania, it has 322mm ground clearance at the diff centre. The double reduction process means a smaller diameter crown wheel is required compared to a single reduction diff typically found on a highway truck.

The principle of how a hub reduction axle operates is essentially the same regardless of the brand. First, power from the engine enters the power-divider head, where the transfer gear distributes driving torque evenly between the front-rear and rear-rear axles. This is achieved because of the differential in the power divider head unit. Next, the torque is transferred partly by a cylindrical spur gear to the front-rear axle's main diff centre and partly through the transfer gear's output shaft to the rear-rear axle's main diff centre via the jackshaft.

The outer wheel end hub reduction gear-set consists of a cylindrical planetary gear, sometimes called a ring gear. In the Scania's case, a floating sun wheel is mounted on the axle shaft end, and five planetary gears attach to the wheel hub. The torque is transferred to these five planetary gears connected to the wheel hub when the main diff centre rotates the axle and sun gear. As the planetary gears rotate, they force against the outer ring gear, which is rigidly fixed to the rear axle casing, consequently gearing down the rotation speed.

Nearly all hub reduction rear axles include a power divider lock that positively connects the two rear axles together to ensure each axle equally receives 50 per cent of the torque. The main rear axle lock fixes the left and right axles together. Once the locks are engaged, the two axles work as one solid axle to ensure each wheel receives an equal share of torque. When the diff locks are engaged, all wheels rotate at the same speed, and consequently, the steering characteristics of the truck is affected.

Typically, diff locks are made of specially hardened steel dog clutches that the driver activates through a dash-mounted switch. The Scania truck has two lamps in the main centre dash to indicate when the diff and power-divider locks are engaged.

In vehicles with the hub reduction gear, the oil circulates between the central gear and hub reduction gear. The hub reduction needs constant lubrication, regular maintenance and oil changes to work. The oil level varies in the central gear located in the outer wheel end depending on how the vehicle has been driven. There is more oil circulating in the central gear at a higher speed and less at a lower speed.

A word of caution here, while the axle's diff lock function promises excellent traction through slippery surfaces, it is crucial to maintain a speed of less than 30kph. It's also essential to ensure that none of the wheels are spinning before the diff locks get engaged.

However, if there is a disadvantage to hub reduction rear axles, it is their tare weight penalty and why they're very rarely specified on a highway truck. And they do require more power to drive than single reduction rear axles, so it's a double whammy on fuel economy and payload for a highway truck. And, for goodness sake, don't abuse them. They are extremely expensive to replace. But if you're serious about heavy haulage, they're a must.

Scania 10x8 Rear Specification

The unique Scania CA8x8EHZ specification includes 4700 mm axle and 1450 mm bogie distances. The Scania fully automated Opticruise gear change system comes with Standard, Power and Off-road modes as well as Ecocruise. The hub-reduction bogie-drive axles deliver impression traction, running a 4.27:1 ratio. The fifth axle is a tag unit fitted at the very rear. Braking is by drums all round backed by traction control, ABS/EBS, while suspension is all steel multi-leaf. The fifth wheel is a heavy-duty Jost DR38C-1 rated to 260 kN.

Scania: Trucking in Australia

Its Hot!
Its Hard!
& Its Heavy!

After shrugging off a 140-tonne payload on a WA gold mine, Scania's mine-spec R620 V8 headed to a QLD coal mine for a 225-tonne run.

Next stop, 292-tonnes in 5-trailers on an iron ore mine in the Pilbara.

Fresh from its tour of the Western Australian Goldfields, where the R620 V8 prime mover was tasked with hauling 140 tonnes of gold ore in four trailers up a haul road, from the extraction point to the crusher, the Scania mine-spec demonstrator truck sent to Mackay in Queensland.

After a brief pit stop en-route at Scania Queensland's Richlands depot to have a beefed-up hydraulics system added, along with a rollover protection system and new antenna bar to carry aerials for a comprehensive telematics system, the truck was soon in action again.

The R 620 was handed over to Craig Briggs, Group Manager for Assets for BIS Industries, and put to the test by hauling four trailers filled with 225 tonnes of washed and processed coal.

The Scania was run for two months, loading coal into giant 3.5m-wide trailers and departing for the railhead tip-off point before returning to reload.

The run was a 38km drive down a mine haul road made of compacted clay, watered daily, though, unlike the Goldfields, the haul road here contained some substantial undulations, including a couple of steep grades named White Hill and Red Hill that knocked the combination's climb speed back to 11km/h. However, on the flat, the combination reached the 74km/h limit with ease and poise.

BIS Industries has pioneered the concept of powered trailers for the mine sites around Australia, where it provides transportation services for mine operators.

For the test Scania, the powered trailer was the second from the front or the middle trailer when the BIS Industries crew ran a visually arresting five-trailer test.

BIS Industries has Five sets of five powered combinations working 24/7 at this particular Queensland facility. The incumbent vehicle is a mine-spec Kenworth C510, explicitly built for the task by the Melbourne-based company for Craig Briggs.

The tri-drive prime movers are powered by a 19-litre Cummins engine and use large 25-inch drive tyres.

The Scania R620, by comparison, is still fitted with its (standard road going) 22.5-inch tyres and is a bogie drive, which, coupled with its factory-supplied fast (4.72) diff in the hub-reduction equipped axles, dents its ability to pull a fully loaded 5-trailer set-up up Red Hill. However, with four trailers, the 225-tonne payload raises no sweat in the Scania's engine bay.

"If we had a lower diff ratio, we'd be able to get the five trailers up the big hill before the tip-off point. And, we'd also be able to crawl through the coal loading choke at a slightly slower speed for smoother loading," says Gary Millewski,

Left: Gary Millewski; grew up on a dairy farm in Minden between Brisbane and Toowoomba. He was driving tractors at ten and milk tankers as soon as he had a licence, which was obtained on his 17th birthday. He is a qualified bodybuilder by training but has spent the better part of 43 years driving and setting-up trucks for others to work in, including a couple of 6-week stints in Zimbabwe. Gary has been with BIS Industries, or Brambles as it was, since 1999.

operator and technical representative within the BIS Industries Asset Support Group, who has been evaluating the Scania at the mine.

Craig Briggs confirms the truck is heading back to Perth for a diff transplant (to a 5.68 ratio), then up to the Pilbara to an iron ore mine near Newman.

"We'll see how it goes in that configuration," he says of the plans to hitch five trailers (one powered) to the R620 and then pull a 292-tonne payload. The GCM would be in the region of 450 tonnes.

"The Scania has been performing above our expectations. In addition, it has performed exceptionally well in the configuration we're running in currently," Craig says.

"The torque the engine produces at low rpm and the transmission coupled to the Retarder certainly eases our use of the service brakes.

"It has been fairly exciting in terms of the fuel it's used for the tonnes we're hauling. But, again, a vast improvement," Craig adds.

"We've only had a couple of drivers on this truck as part of this assessment, but the operator that has done most of the work, Gary Millewski, has been suitably impressed with the truck's performance and handling and the comfort in the cab."

Craig confirms that driver acceptance is one of the main areas the company focuses on, along with safety and performance. He also praises the Scania Mining and Resources Division's team led by Robert Taylor.

"Since we started working with Scania, Rob Taylor and his team have been more than accommodating in what we wanted to do with the prime mover, (such as) some minor alterations to suit our application and our task," Craig says.

The ability of Scania's Hub Reduction ADA 1501P axle housings with RBP 835 gears to absorb the torque and convert it to usable traction effectively, enables the Scania truck to run a bogie drive efficiently to haul the massive multi combination rig.

Traditionally these trailers were towed by tri-drive or purpose built OFF-Road prime movers with larger expensive drive tyres.

Scania: Trucking in Australia

"One of the benefits of the Scania Prime mover is the advanced technology that we can tap into for our own on-board telematics. This assists the driver in obtaining the best use of the truck. But, more importantly, for us to understand what the truck is going through so, we can match the performance of both.

"(Due to) the cost of a prime mover, we need to ensure that we have the driver trained to get the maximum from him, and also the performance of the truck, so both go hand in hand. The telematics in the Scania takes us a long way towards getting 100 per cent efficiency," Craig says.

Working on the coalmine, pulling 225 tonnes of coal has not been a problem for the beefy Scania over 6000km of testing. With its high torque – low revving V8 engine, the R 620 has been a perfect match for the task.

The Scania three-pedal Opticruise and Scania Retarder have played a key role in winning over long-time BIS Industries' test driver Gary Millewski, who has been enjoying the driving experience.

Gary's job is to evaluate new equipment and then set it up for use on the many BIS Industries' worksites around Australia. He's been working with Craig for more than a dozen years.

Gary has experimented with the Scania Opticruise automated gear changing system and the powered trailer controls to harmoniously synthesise the grunt of both motors to ensure that neither is under strain, even when grinding up the big red hill before the tip-off point.

"The Opticruise does give very smooth gear changes and has an excellent ability to hold a gear. I like the ability to be able to manually drop back a couple of gears ahead of the approach to the big hills so that the engine is working hard initially, and I can let the revs fall back as the truck climbs the hill without having to change gear again.

"I will usually come back to 2nd early and allow the truck to climb the hill, using its torque. I prefer the truck not to change gear on the climb as you can lose momentum, and with the powered trailer. Also, you don't want both of them changing gear at the same time," Gary says. "Driving this way means I don't have to be extracting 100 per cent power from both engines on the climb, which saves on wear and tear and stress on the engine. You can even hear the fan cut out on the climb, which shows the engine is not working that hard.

"With the new differentials, the truck will have even better gradeability. "One of the first things I noticed about the Scania was that it has very direct steering," Gary says. "It is quite different from the many turns lock-to-lock you have with bonneted trucks. As a result, you quickly learn to trust the truck, and you don't need to chase the steering.

"I like the fact that there's no effort in driving this truck. You can sit back and let the truck do the driving. You're not working the gears, just allowing the high torque and low revs to do the work for you.

"I like the live PTO, as well," Gary says. "It is a much better system than a transmission-driven PTO because it is still pumping even if you have the clutch in. Also, we need the hydraulic drive for the tip bins, and we only tip while we are stationary, so the live PTO means we can have hydraulic power all the time.

"It did take me a while to get used to a cab over again, but the visibility is good," he says.

Low fuel use has impressed both Gary and Craig, with the 225-tonne payload across four trailers consuming around 97 litres per 100 km.

> "I like the fact that there's no effort in driving this truck. You can sit back and let the truck do the driving."

In typical Scania style, the R620 Sleeper Cab has charmed the test driver with its spaciousness, comfort, quietness, and features such as the built-in fridge freezer.

"I admit I was sceptical at first that the Scania on its smaller wheels would be able to do the job, but it has done well," he says.

"I call this Scania my metric Mack," Gary says. "In the early 1970s, I drove a Mack that had so much torque it rarely needed a gear change. Some Macks of the time even had Scania-Vabis stamped on their engine blocks.

"What we particularly like is that there is a lot of telemetry in the vehicle, so we can analyse how it performs to a very high degree. We keep a close eye on fuel consumption and wear and tear," Gary says.

According to Robert Taylor, General Manager of Scania Australia's Mining and Resources Division, the BIS Industries test has shown that the R 620 is tough enough for the job.

"We made a few changes ahead of the test deployment to the BIS mine near Mackay, in line with the request from BIS Industries. We were happy to make the changes, and the result is that the vehicle has done an exceptional job pulling 225 tonnes of coal in four trailers. The testing Gary has done with the truck now shows that it can cope with four trailers and is now ready for five.

"Once we have the differentials swapped back in Perth, this R620 will be ready for the Pilbara and 292 tonnes of iron ore. The Pilbara test will be an excellent way of showing off the core strength of the Scania product. There are not many places in the world where you can pull five trailers and not

many places where you have a 292-tonne payload, but this vehicle will indeed be up to the task and with all the benefits for operators of ease of deployment. The R620 is entirely road legal, so we have been driving it bobtail from state to state across Australia for its demonstration duties, with none of the fuss or bother associated with bespoke mining machinery. It also runs on regular-sized tyres, significantly reducing running costs and parts supply complexity.

"These are just some of the reasons why a Scania mine vehicle makes so much sense for operators around Australia and the region," Robert says.

TRUCK SPECIFICATIONS

Model:	Scania R 620 CA6x4 EHZ
Engine:	Scania DC16 730 16-Litre V8
Horsepower:	730 hp (537)kw @1800 RPM
Torque:	2581lb/ft (3500Nm) @ 1000-1400 RPM
Gearbox:	Scania GRS0925R 14-speed Overdrive
Retarder:	Scania R3500
PTO:	Rear EG652P
Alternator:	Scania 24V 150amp
Compressor:	Knorr 720, twin cylinder, 800 L/min with air dryer
Front Axles:	Scania AM 420S
Front Suspension:	3 x 29 Parabolic 7,500kg with anti-roll bar
Rear Axles:	Scania ADA 1501P axle housings with RBP 835 gears
Rear Axle Ratio:	4.72 with diff locks to both axles
Rear Suspension:	Scania 4-Bag, 21,000 kg
Brakes:	Scania electronically controlled drum brakes
Safety:	EBS with integrated ABS and traction control
Interior:	Velour Trim
Seats:	Premium driver's seat with armrests
Bumper:	Powder coated double tube steel
Battery Box:	2x12V, 180 amp Chassis mount LH side
Fuel Tank:	1 x 400L R/H side
Adblue tank:	1 x 70L L/H side
Trailers:	J Smith and Sons, Gympie, QLD
Capacity:	55-60 tonnes each
Payload 4-trailers:	225 tonnes Processed Coal
Payload 5-trailers:	292 tonnes Processed Coal
GCM 4-trailers:	360 tonnes,
GCM 5-trailers:	430 tonnes
Max Cruising Speed:	74km/h
Typical max grades of the hills:	4 %
4-Trailer Combination max grade:	8%,
5-Trailer Combination max grade:	6%
Typical Ambient Operating Temp:	32°C

Scania: Trucking in Australia

ON THE WAY TO THE FUTURE
AUTONOMOUS TRUCKING

The move to autonomous transport is underway. It is, however, a generational shift and not an overnight, sudden change. It is one that will take time. And, for the most part any changes will be gradual in a way that will see a natural shift from the traditional operations we know today to newer transport solutions.

Rio Tinto is no stranger to autonomous vehicles having pioneered the use of automation in the mining industry, with the largest fleet of driverless trucks, the world's first fully-autonomous heavy haul, long distance rail network, and fully autonomous production drills.

Recently the mining company commenced trailing a Scania XT 8x4 autonomous tipper truck working separately from Dampier's active operations. During the early stage, a safety driver rides in the vehicle to observe the truck's performance and, if necessary, intervenes. In subsequent phases, additional autonomous Scania trucks will be added to develop vehicle-vehicle awareness and intelligent fleet supervisory controls.

Rio Tinto head of Productivity & Technical Support, Rob Atkinson said, "We're pleased to be trialling this technology in trucks that are smaller than our traditional haul trucks. This has the potential to give us more flexibility in the way we operate in a number of areas across Rio Tinto. We have seen automation create safer and more efficient operations in our business and this is a next step in evaluating options for delivering further improvements through the use of technology."

Björn Winblad, Head of Scania Mining said, "Mining sites, given their high vehicle utilisation rates are ideal for testing new autonomous technology. The industry can reap the safety and productivity benefits of automation, and the experience gained here will be instrumental in developing fully autonomous solutions for other transport applications. It is very encouraging to note that the truck has been performing in a safe manner and in accordance with expectations with regards to the operations."

How will autonomous trucks affect the drivers?

Scania are quick to allay any fears that automation will lead to mass unemployment of transport drivers, especially given there is a global driver shortage that has only become more acute in recent years. But secondly that drivers will still be required for the foreseeable future while the technology matures.

The Five Levels of Automation

Level-1
The first level of automation. When a vehicle features a single automated system for driver assistance, such as accelerating (cruise control). Adaptive cruise control, where the vehicle can be kept at a safe distance behind the next vehicle also qualifies as Level-1 because the human driver must control the other aspects of driving such as steering and braking.

Level-2
This means advanced driver assistance systems (ADAS). At this level the vehicle can control both steering and acceleration or deceleration. Yet the automation falls short of self-driving because a human sits in the driver's seat and can take control of the vehicle at any time.

Level-3
From a technological perspective the jump from Level-2 to Level 3 is substantial. Yet from a human perspective subtle if not negligible. Level-3 vehicles have "environmental detection" capabilities and can make informed decisions for themselves, such as accelerating past a slow-moving vehicle. But they still require a human override. The driver must remain alert and ready to take control if the system is unable to execute the task.

Level-4:
Highly Automated Driving vehicles with Level-4 Autonomy are capable of driving fully autonomously in proper settings without the assistance or intervention of a human driver.

Level-5
Fully Autonomous Driving are Level-5 vehicles and don't have steering wheels or accelerator or brake pedals as they do not require human attention because the "dynamic driving task" is eliminated.

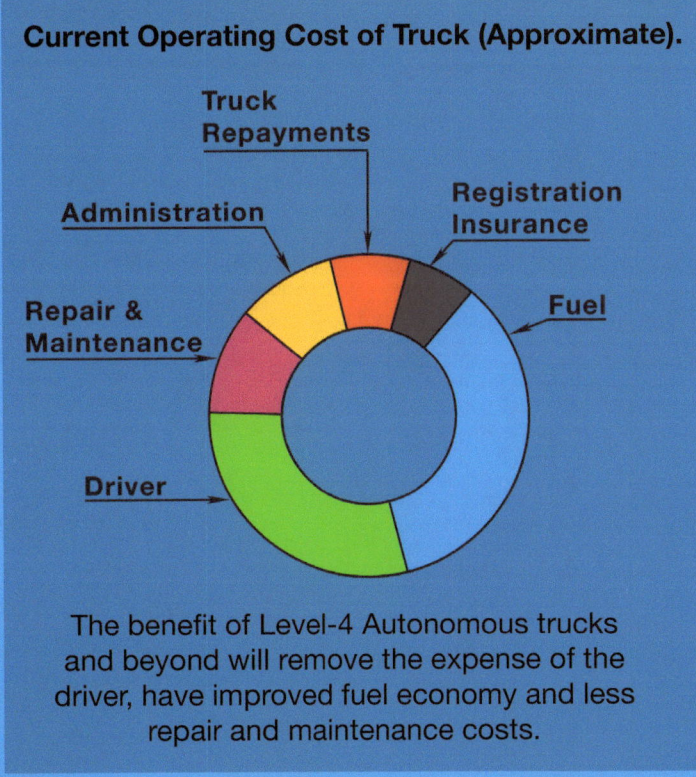

Current Operating Cost of Truck (Approximate).

The benefit of Level-4 Autonomous trucks and beyond will remove the expense of the driver, have improved fuel economy and less repair and maintenance costs.

Although even beyond mass adoption of autonomous trucks, it's apparent that local drivers will be necessary for the first and last part of loading and unloading in any hub-to-hub transport journey.

Autonomous Advantage

In any most forms of freight transport, economic and ecological arguments are driving the push towards Automation. There is no denying that self-driving trucks can cover longer distances without requiring a break and drastically reduce the high personnel costs, which after fuel costs account for the largest proportion of the total operating costs of a truck.

In addition, automated driving leads to lower fuel consumption and thus reduces the impact on the environment. At the same time, less damage also means fewer breakdowns and lower repair costs. At Rio Tinto they anticipate fuel savings in excess of nine per cent for their Level-4 Autonomous Scania, and even more when they go to full driverless operation.

Nevertheless, autonomous trucks present a viable solution to one of the biggest challenges facing the transportation industry world-wide, being the massive increase in driver shortages. According to the Australian Government's

labour market insights website, the average age of an Australian truck driver, at the time of writing, is 48. Alarmingly out of the 140,000 odd truck drivers nationally, more than 20,000 drivers are leaving the industry annually, while the industry is only attracting up 16,000 new drivers per year.

For Scania however, the ongoing autonomous integration in mining operations like Rio Tinto's Damper Salt project is paving the way forward for the company, customers and industry. Because the future will belong to autonomous trucks.

Scania R730 8x4 loading 171 tonne of iron ore at Iron Valley in Pilbara region of Western Australia. This truck runs a 12-hour shift from Port Hedland to Iron Valley and return, seven days and nights per week. The iron ore is unloaded at the port. The full story of this hard working R730 Scania features in **Great Australian Road Trains -Collector's Issue #1.**

Contributor's Acknowledgment

Page:	Title:	Author:	Photography:
Page-1	Front Truck Graphic		
Page: 2-3	Poster - Milk Tanker		Howard Shanks
Page: 4-5	Contents		
Page: 6-11	LB80 Restoration	Howard Shanks	Howard Shanks
Page: 12-13	Super Swede	Reporoduction	Truckin' Life April 1978
Page: 14-17	L111 Restored	Scania Australia	Charlie Suriano
Page: 18-21	T143H Diggin' It	Scania Australia	Charlie Suriano
Page: 22-23	Evolution of Dash	Howard Shanks/Scania Australia	Howard Shanks/Scania Australia
Page: 24-29	R560 PBS Double	Howard Shanks	Howard Shanks
Page: 30-37	General Access	Howard Shanks	Howard Shanks
Page:38:-45	All Wheel Drive XT	Howard Shanks	Howard Shanks
Page: 46-49	A Long Haul to the Top	Scania Australia	Scania Australia
Page: 50-54	R730 in the Hardwood	Scania Australia	Charlie Suriano
Page: 55-57	The Good Fuel	Scania Australia	Paul Kane
Page: 58-63	Pumped Up P380	Howard Shanks	Howard Shanks
Page: 64-67	Tonka Truck	Scania Australia	B& J Catalano
Page: 68-73	Custom Scania	Scania Australia	Charlie Suriano
Page: 74-79	R730 Floats On	Scania Australia	Charlie Suriano
Page: 80-81	Drake Steering Widener	Howard Shanks	Charlie Suriano/Howard Shanks
Page: 82-89	Low Logger & Traction	Scania Australia	Charlie Suriano
Page: 90-95	The Grain Train	Scania Australia	Paul Kane
Page: 96-99	Opticruise G33	Howard Shanks	Scania Australia
Page: 100-105	Packing on the Payload	Howard Shanks	Howard Shanks
Page: 106-110	Turning Heads	Scania Australia	Paul Kane
Page: 111 -117	Movin On R730	Scania Australia	Paul Kane
Page: 118 -125	Clean & Green	Howard Shanks	Howard Shanks
Page: 126 -127	Scania Mining Trucks	Howard Shanks	
Page: 128 -133	Hub Reduction Diffs Explained	Howard Shanks/Scania Australia	Paul Kane
Page: 134 -141	Its Hot! Its Hard! & Its Heavy!	Scania Australia	Charlie Suriano
Page: 142-147	On the way to the Future	Howard Shanks/Scania Australia	Paul Kane

www.ingramcontent.com/pod-product-compliance
Lightning Source LLC
Chambersburg PA
CBHW041518220426
43667CB00002B/30